SHORT WALKS
IN THE
CAIRNGORMS

ERNEST CROSS

SHORT WALKS
IN THE
CAIRNGORMS

By

Ernest Cross

Luath Press Ltd.
Barr, Ayrshire KA26 9TN

First Edition 1991

Revised Edition 1992

Revised Edition 1994

For
Alexandra Sophie McDonald
from Grandpa, who is waiting impatiently
for the day when he can introduce
you to the delights of
walking, especially
walking in the
Cairngorms.

Designed and Typeset by Luath Press, Barr, Ayrshire.
Printed and Bound by Dynevor Printing Co. Llandybie, Dyfed.

ACKNOWLEDGEMENTS

It is something of a mystery to me why Phil and Ben, and sometimes Jane and Alf, continue to walk with me. I am forever stopping to take photographs and to make notes: I often change my mind and the route: I tend to hang about in uncomfortable places waiting for wild animals that just won't show, and I do occasionally go where people seem not to have gone before. These things can have unfortunate side effects, like cold and wet feet, and missed meals, but they can also lead to some secluded and ineffably beautiful places, and this is what makes it all worthwhile.

It is unwise to go it alone in the Cairngorms, and I gratefully acknowledge the support and understanding of my companions, and also of my wife. Without them, this book would probably not have been written.

At Loch Morlich Youth Hostel, the Wardens have changed, but nothing else has, and I feel that I have known Phil and Gail for donkey's years.

Maureen Riley took the candid photograph that was the basis for the drawing of 'The Watcher by the Shore.'

MAP NOTES

The sketch maps indicate direction, terrain and scale. They are intended to be an aid to route planning in conjunction with a proper map, but they should be adequate on their own in clear weather conditions. It is assumed that all walkers will take note of local weather information, and it is emphasised that inexperienced walkers should not go on to the hills if bad weather is forecast.

The Visitors Guide to Rothiemurchus is a valuable aid for walks in that area. It is freely available at the Visitors Centre in Inverdruie, and at various other points in Rothiemurchus.

The Forestry Commission Wayfaring map provides unequalled detail for parts of The Queen's Forest.

The whole area is covered by Bartholomew's Sheet 51, Grampian, and by the following OS maps:

Cairngorm Tourist Map, 1 inch : 1 mile.
Grantown and Cairngorm. 1 : 50000 (not walks 14/15)
Aviemore and the Cairngorms. 1 : 25000

National Grid References are used in walk descriptions.

CONTENTS

Watchers by the shore

FOREWORD

One day, last year, a lady went into the Information Centre in Aviemore and asked for a guide book for some local walks. She said she wanted to do a short hill walk, and she was offered *Walks in the Cairngorms*. 'No,' she said, 'I have looked at that, and all the hill walks are too long or too strenuous.' She was then offered Mr. Laird's book of *Spey Valley Walks*. This, too, was declined because 'There are no hill walks in it.' As there were no other books, the lady was directed to Highland Guides to see if she could hire someone to take her on the hill for the afternoon.

At that point I should have interrupted and earned myself some easy money, but I was too slow as usual.

The definition of a short walk could prompt a long, acrimonious, inconclusive and totally pointless discussion. It is certainly not a few weeks in the mountains of Nuristan, but it is a perambulation to the pub; it is a half day's walk; it is a bird-watching wander through the woods; it is five miles over the mountains; it is a saunter in the forest; it is an afternoon on the hill; it is a quiet meander along a river bank; it is an idle mooch around a marsh; above all, it is what each individual decides it is.

This book has all these walks, and then some more, and it could be just the book that the lady wanted but could not buy. Life being what it is, she will probably never see a copy, but, if she does, she should know that I am very grateful to her for suggesting it.

INTRODUCTION

Humans have been walking for as long as they have had legs, but for most of human history, people have walked from place to place simply because they have had to. Walking for leisure and pleasure are generally thought to be modern concepts, but they are not all that new, and there must always have been some people who enjoyed walking for its own sake. Indeed, at the beginning of the 17th century Thomas Coryate walked to Venice on a sort of pedestrian precursor of the Grand Tour. His journey took him through much of Europe, and the resulting book, *Coryate's Crudities,* is an entertaining, and, at times, hilarious story of his travels. It was published in 1608. Few books on the subject were published for a long time after that, and walkers as a class were quite unpopular later in the 17th century. On the whole they were regarded as vagabonds, and they were treated, or maltreated, accordingly.

It was not until the late 18th century, when people like Wordsworth, Hazlitt, Coleridge, de Quincey and Southey got going, that walking in the country purely for pleasure became a recognised leisure pursuit, and for a long time only a fortunate few could enjoy it.

One of the problems, of course, was that until quite recently the majority of people had neither the time nor the means. There was an upsurge of hiking in the 1930's -- the Ramblers Association dates from then -- but the real explosion came after the end of World War II, and less drudgery, more leisure and more money may be some of the most significant benefits of the new industrial revolution that has been going on for the last fifty years. Whatever the reason, more people than ever before now regularly enjoy the pleasures that can only be had from staring nature in the face whilst travelling on one's own two feet.

The countryside around Aviemore is an ideal place to do this, but it is quite untypical of the country elsewhere in Britain. In fact, the very title of this book is something of a paradox, since some would hold that it is impossible to have a short walk in the Cairngorms. Well, it *is* possible: read on!

The Cairngorms are unique amongst British mountains in terms of altitude, of climate, and of scale. Everything is impressively large, the maps are notable for their lack of marked paths, and it is all rather different from much of the other hill country in Britain. The individual Cairngorm peaks are also noted for their remoteness, and this poses a major problem for hill walkers. There is little alternative to a long trek in and out, and this problem rules out much of the region as a place for short hill walks.

That is why most of the hill walks in this book are concentrated in and around Glen More, where the ski road and the chairlift have made access to the plateau and to Cairngorm summit quick, easy, and relatively cheap. Although still much criticised, there is no doubt that these facilties are a great boon to most visitors, and by concentrating traffic in this way they have also taken the pressure off other areas, and that can't be bad. It is a bit like Loch Garten and the ospreys.

This book is about where to walk, and it is not about how, or why. But there are some practical points, not at all obvious to the tyro, which might usefully be explained. Most walkers are probably naturalists at heart, which means that they have an interest in natural things, but not necessarily a scientific interest. They just want to enjoy all that a walk can offer, and that includes the varied wildlife. The following principles, once understood and then practiced, can add greatly to the pleasures of any day in the country.

The vast majority of people see and hear little of the wildlife of the hills and woodlands, and most conclude that wildlife is scarce or extinct. It is not, and one's every step is carefully observed because most walkers telegraph their coming for many miles ahead. First, there is the matter of dress. It is popularly supposed that a red or orange anorak renders rescue more certain if one is lost or injured on the hill. This may be true, but brightly coloured clothing is easily seen by all the wild things, and they instantly go to ground or depart. The muted hues and soft shades of traditional tweeds and hunting tartans are not a sign of sartorial restraint -- witness the splendour of the dress plaids -- nor do they signify reckless tendencies on the part of deer stalkers, shepherds and other working hillmen. They were a practical response to the need for unobtrusive dress by a people whose very livelihood was tied to a successful hunt or pillage. The principle remains, and brown, beige and 'cowpat' green are all good

colours for the country. Tweeds are in vogue again, and the newly ubiquitous 'Barbour' is a boon. Untreated quiet cottons, like Grenfell cloth, are worn by many serious naturalists.

Other factors are noise and vibration. To see wildlife during a country walk it is necessary to be quiet, to tread lightly, walk softly and refrain from chatter. Try to develop a 'third eye' which senses what is behind the next tree, and don't be in such a tearing hurry. The seasoned nature watcher tends to spend a lot of time loitering, apparently doing nothing much at all, but that extra hour on the walk can be quite exhausting as well as most rewarding: sustained concentration is hard work. Small groups are always preferable to large parties, and it is an advantage to be walking into the wind. All these factors add up to one thing: minimal disturbance to the natural inhabitants of the countryside. Please remember that it is their world as well as ours, and that they live here whilst we are merely visitors. It is really just a form of courtesy; try it, and be pleasantly surprised by the difference it will make.

One last point: with the single exception of Loch Avon, all the walks can be reversed, and the differences in aspect are so great that this effectively doubles the number of walks.

LOCHS AND LOCHANS

Haggis and Hogmanay are synonymous with Scotland, and so are lochs and lochans. The mountain scenery of this enchanted land is world renowned, and a mountain scene is always better when it is set off by a loch. In Scotland, one is almost spoiled for choice, and there is a stretch of water close at hand virtually everywhere in the Highlands.

The natural lochs of Scotland are usually features of the following kinds:

Rift Lakes, which are formed by earth movement or faulting. The Great Glen, and Loch Ness, are examples known to everyone.

Glacial Lakes, cut and scraped by the chiseling action of the moving ice. Loch Avon and Loch Einich are classic examples.

Kettle Holes, formed when an ice plug, embedded in sand and gravel, melted and left behind a water filled cavity. Loch Morlich is a perfect specimen.

Glacial and rift lakes tend to be long in relation to their width, and they are usually steep sided and very deep. The quoted lochs are extreme examples, but most lochs are glacial lakes, and will therefore have these characteristics to some degree. It should be noted that a type of small glacial lake, usually round in shape, and rarely deep, is often found in rocky corries. It is always called a lochan in Scotland. More usually, lochans lie in areas of glacial debris, and are, in effect, large ponds. Kettle holes are much less common, and they tend to be squarish, or virtually circular. They are usually quite shallow, and often lie apart from the mountains. Loch Leven is probably the best generally-known example. There is another kind of still water pool called a peat hole, which looks like a lochan, but is not glacial, and is certainly not a kettle hole. Why and how they are formed is a bit of a mystery, but they tend to crop up in areas of sphagnum peat blanket, when the peat is locally washed away. There are several examples near Ryvoan Bothy. The adjacent Loch a'Gharbh Choire looks like a very large peat hole, but it is probably artificial. It could have been created when the stream was dammed to form a reservoir for logging operations in the 18th and 19th centuries. A little dam remains, and the lochan would probably dry up if it were removed.

There is not much sense in trying to explain what constitutes a loch, or how lochs differ from lochans: the differences are debatable, and somewhat academic. We all know one when we see one, and we all have our own ideas, so what would be the point? The important thing is to recognise that lochs and lochans are fascinating and captivating features in their own right. They are all different, and all have something to offer the interested visitor. They attract fishers, both human and avian. They have a distinct and distinctly varied fauna and flora, which appeals to all sorts of naturalists, and they are as varied in their appearance as they are in their location. They are photogenic to a high degree.

There is a great deal of real pleasure and a rare contentment to be had from simply sitting on the banks of any sort of loch on a balmy late-spring day. The sky seems very high, the clouds float gently, and there is a particular sort of freshness in the air. There is usually the sound of water running somewhere close by, and an occasional 'plop' as a hungry trout leaps out of the water in pursuit of a passing gnat. Sunlight flashes on the irridescent bodies of the damsel flies, and the buzz and drone of busy bees and midges mingle with the gentle chobbeling of sundry waterfowl which are rooting in the reeds at the water margins. All these sights and sounds emphasise the sense of isolation from the rest of a rather frantic mankind. It is sheer bliss.

The following seven walks visit some of the many lochs and lochans in the area. None of the lochs is very big, but all are extremely pleasant places. All but one of the walks are decidedly gentle, but the visit to Loch Avon, which, incidentally, is pronounced 'arn', although of modest mileage, does require good weather, a full day, and a lot of stamina. For these reasons, the walk to this loch should be undertaken only by fit, healthy and fairly experienced hill-walkers.

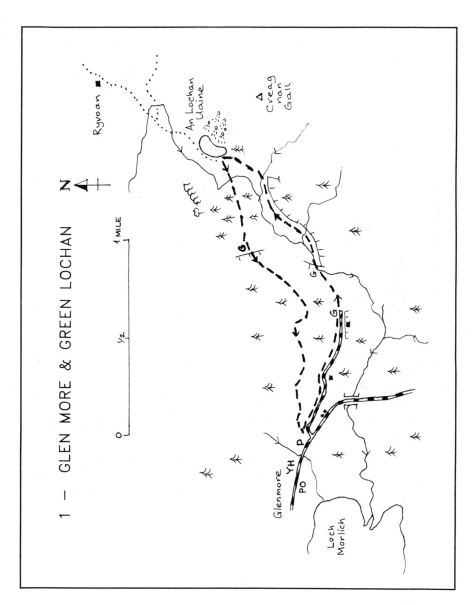

1 – GLEN MORE & GREEN LOCHAN

Ryvoan ■

An Lochan Uaine

△ Creag nan Gall

N

1 MILE

½

0

Glenmore YH
P
PO

Loch Morlich

1 -- GLEN MORE AND THE GREEN LOCHAN

Glenmore is a tiny and unpretentious hamlet at the NE corner of Loch Morlich. It comprises a Post Office-cum-Cafe-cum-General Store, a Youth Hostel, the Reindeer House, the Forestry Commission Office and a chapel (all welcome and all welcoming for a good sing on a Sunday evening). There is also a group of foresters' houses. In the appropriate seasons the resident population is augmented by the transients at the Youth Hostel, on the caravan/camp site, and in the few B. and B. houses. These are often people who come one week for a week and want to stay on without really knowing why. They all go home, of course, but only after developing a tendency to keep coming back year after year.

Glenmore is a perfect compromise, because it is relatively close to the fleshpots of Aviemore, but is remote enough to be blissfully quiet between tea time and breakfast time. It is very close to the mountains, and is an ideal place for almost any sort of outdoor holiday. One wonders why the Aviemore Centre was not built here instead -- perhaps the planners got it right for once? The ambience is overwhelmingly one of peace and tranquility, which rubs off on the visitors. People who, at home, would hurry by without a glance, are inclined to pause and discuss the weather (inevitably), the fishing (always so-so), the walking (never too strenuous) or almost anything remote from the monotony of their normal but seemingly all too abnormal everyday world. If it sounds like some sort of primitive Heaven, or haven in the Highlands, be assured that it is; and be thankful for simply being there.

It would be simpler if it were called 'Kinlochmorlich', but it isn't, and Glenmore, the hamlet, should not be confused with Glen More, and to avoid confusion with its more illustrous namesake, the Great Glen, it may be well to explain that this Glen More is the open-ended valley that extends, roughly, some three or four miles from Ryvoan to the hamlet of Glenmore. It is traversed from end to end by the Thieves Road -- the ancient *Rathad nam Mearlach* -- and it has the Kincardine Hills on one hand and the Cairngorms on the other. It is a very small area of very great beauty, and it is worthy of more than the cursory interest usually displayed by transients en route to places of larger size and greater renown. This gentle walk of some four miles need take no more than a short afternoon, and it may even be accomplished as an after dinner stroll on a long summer evening. Some folk can make it last all day, and the enjoyment increases in proportion. It provides a lot of very good value for very little effort.

Start from the car park by the Forestry Commission Office, which is just beyond the Youth Hostel, and on the same side of the road (NH970098). On the green here there is a large erratic boulder set in an area of paving, and with a few planted alpines which have survived the early morning browsing of the deer. This is the Norwegian Stone, and it is a hallowed memorial to the very many Norwegians of Kompani Linge, who lived and trained in this district, and who subsequently died on operations during the last war. The present Youth Hostel was the Operations Centre for the famous Telemark Raid and the Norwegian Hostel, on the road to New Glenmore Lodge, is built on the site of the old Commando Barracks. There is a timeless air about the memorial, and it is refreshing to see that some people still care -- there are always fresh flowers at the base of the stone.

Take the path over the green, past the end of Reindeer House, and follow the stretch of asphalt road to the outdoor pursuits school at Glemore Lodge. This modern building has taken the name which rightly belongs to the Loch Morlich Youth Hostel, the old hunting

NORWEGIAN STONE – Glenmore

lodge of the Dukes of Richmond and Gordon. It has been pointed out that feet are always the last things to tire when traversing fell and moorland. Conversely, they are always the first things to tire when walking on tarmac, and the truth of this assertion will be apparent during this first half mile or so if you walk down the road. Take heart, for most of the way the road has a foresters' scrape on the left hand side, and there is plenty of interest along there. There are milk-, butter-, louse- and other worts, and there are newts in the puddles of the tyre ruts. Where do they come from, and where do they go? The newts, that is.

Just beyond the lodge, by the locked gate, one or two cars can be parked in a little lay-by. Beyond the gate there is a rough forest road, and a complete change in the character of the country. The serried ranks of close-planted alien conifers are replaced by a much more open and interesting landscape. Low mounds, with birch scrub and marshy stretches in between, are plentifully dotted here and there with small Scots pines. The mounds are moraines, left behind when a large glacial lake emptied through Ryvoan. The marshy patches are all that remains of the residual lochans that originally spattered the area, but have since either drained away or silted up.

The trees here are really quite a rarity: they are some of the few remnants of the old Caledonian Forest. They grow high up on the flanks of the hills that bound the pass immediately ahead, and the tree line is well above the 1500 foot contour which is normally the limit for successful tree growth in Britain. This indicates a very sheltered site, but because of the very short growing season and poor soil fertility, the trees, whilst very old, are very small. This is a happy accident, for very large trees would be a mite overpowering in this intimate little glen.

About a mile further along the track, at the margin of the Queen's Forest, the impressive face of Creag Nan Gall rises on the right. It marks the end of a low outlier from the main Cairngorm ridge, but, geologically, this spur is not part of the Cairngorms at all. They are granite hills, and the rock exposed here is a form of granulite, and masses of the cold grey stone can be seen in the screes cascaded down the hillside on the right. The Creag is probably a separated chunk of the Kincardine Hills, and they, in turn, are possibly a detached arm of the Monadhliaths. It is all something of a rocky hotch-potch. As might now be guessed, the divide, which we call the Pass of Ryvoan, is a glacial feature, and it is an extreme example of an overflow channel.

An Lochan Uaine has a dramatic setting backed by the rugged screes and trees of the Creag. Many regard this as the most beautiful of the many 'Green Lochans' of the Cairngorms. It is certainly a delightful spot in which to laze away the odd half hour on a bonny day. It gets its name because the complete lack of marine vegetation, coupled with minute flakes of mica in the clear water, make it reflect

-14-

the colour of its rocky bed, and the water is a lovely emerald green. Sometimes, in early summer, the water close inshore looks like custard. This is caused by the accumulation of pollen from the surrounding trees.

Leaving the lochan, take the faint track that strikes back across the valley towards the tree-clad hillside of Creag Loisgte. The uphill path is narrow, and, in places, very steep. It also has a wealth of snags, like concealed rocks and old tree roots, to trip up the unwary, so do not try to sight-see on the move. Be sensible, and stop often to enjoy the view down the glen and across the great northern corries to Chalamain and beyond. This short climb can be a delight for the naturalist, and many interesting plants and birds may be seen on the warm and very sheltered hill. The path eventually emerges onto a

pink-gritted forest road, which is followed down to the car park, and the many cleared rides to the left offer pleasant views down to the Ryvoan track and beyond. It may be noted that some of the more mature trees are really quite beautiful, particularly the blue spruces. There seem to be many varieties of this conifer, and some of them have an unusual weeping form. So Forestry Commission Plantings can be quite attractive, after all! The trees here are also home to many crested tits, and a chance to see these tiny rarities should add to the attractions of this delightful walk.

OSPREY

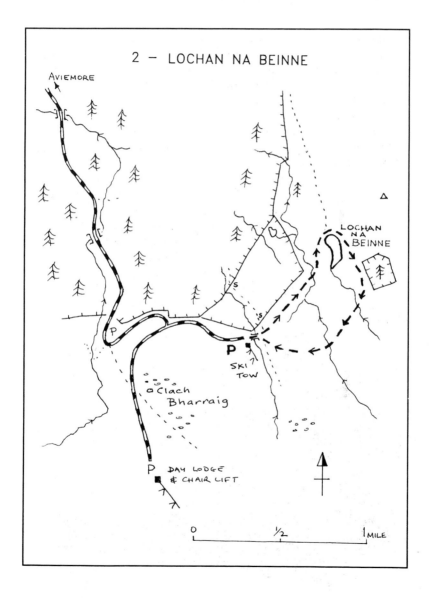

2 — LOCHAN NA BEINNE

2 - Lochan na Beinne

This little lochan nestles in a peaty hollow on the moor below the N ridge at the unfashionable end of Cairngorm, and it should be of interest to fishermen because the trout, although not large, are numerous and quite wild. It was one of the favourite fishing lochs of a dear friend who lived in the area and fished all its waters for many years. The gullies of the little burns that drain corries Ciste, and Laogh Mor and Beag, all have to be crossed en-route, and they provide quiet and private sun traps for the indolent. These are places in which to idle away the odd half hour looking at plants, watching birds, hoping to see a mountain hare, or simply doing nothing at all.

Follow the A951 to Cairngorm, but park at Coire na Ciste (NH998074), and not at the main car park. Go to the far end of the car park, climb down the wooden steps near the ski-tow pylon, cross the little bridge and contour over the moor, going in a roughly NE direction and keeping to the right of the fence and slightly above the narrow, but squelchy, shallow flat on the right. After about a third of a mile of undulating heather the lochan will be seen, beyond and below the stream that drains Coire Laogh Mor.

These watery gullies, which at first sight look rather drab, are really full of interest. They may contain, for instance, curlews, grouse, deer, other smaller mammals, and reptiles. The variety of plants is not large, but they are as diverse as golden saxifrage and mountain sorrel, and whilst none of the plants is a real rarity, they form interesting and intriguing combinations.

From the lochan go uphill, towards the experimental tree plantation, and contour back over the moor to the car park. This is a rough but interesting stretch of country where cloudberries bloom amongst massed cow, crow and bearberries, and the starry flowers of bog asphodel add little spots of sunshine on the greyest of days. This walk of some two miles will easily occupy a morning or an afternoon.

It is a fact of life that guide books are nearly always out of date, and this one is no exception. The first edition was no sooner off the press than the Forestry Commission decided to extend Queen's Forest and plough and plant most of the ground of the original walk. This revision is, perhaps, an improvement.

Dotterel

3 – LOCH MORLICH

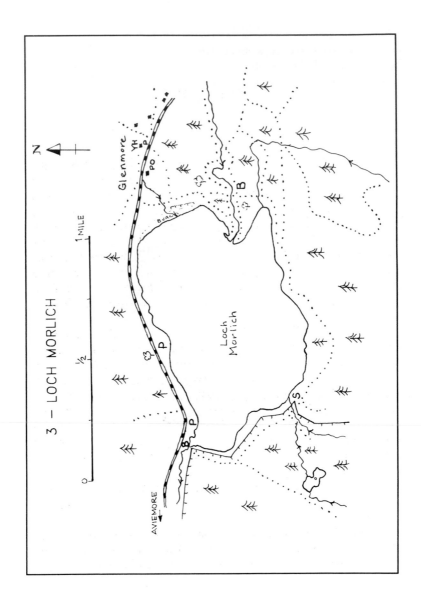

3 -- LOCH MORLICH

Loch Morlich is, apparently, a classic example of a kettle-hole. For those, the majority of normal folk, unfamiliar with the more esoteric jargon of the geologists, this means that it is a water-filled depression that marks the final resting place of a very large lump of ice -- the dying remnant of the last glacier in Glen More. Some 10,000 years ago the ice lump lay like a monstrous rotting tooth whilst the continuing thaw slowly embedded it in an aggregate of mud, sand and gravel. When the ice finally melted away, the resultant cavity formed the loch. A crude description for a very complex process, but, hopefully, it does explain how it happened.

It is amazing that geologists can be sure of this, because it happened such a long time ago, but it does account for the peculiar contours of the bottom of the loch, which is generally shallow, except at the E end, where a submarine cliff, with a slope of 1 in 4, falls 50 feet into the hole. The geological processes continue, and the edge of the cliff is advancing slowly westward as the Allt Mor continually washes in a fresh supply of sand and gravel. Several acres of beach have been added this century, and the rate of change is so rapid that differences can be noticed from year to year. One day, perhaps, the loch will be no more: it will be filled up with detritus from the hills, and Cairngorm, perhaps, will be by then a mere shadow of its present self, and people will walk on it, instead of up it.

Judged solely by the map, the loch must seem to offer little of interest to the walker. One side is bounded by the ski-road, and forestry roads flank two other sides. Only at the Allt Mor beach-head are there minor paths expressly for walking on. As with many other things in this world, appearances are deceptive, and the area is full of interest. The loch is another piece in the geological jig-saw that has produced such a varied and attractive landscape.

The loch has an appeal of its own, and it has a wonderful setting in the old pine woods at the foot of the great northern corries of Cairngorm. The best times for a walk here are early or late in the day, and early morning has the edge so far as birdlife is concerned. Deer, both red and roe, seem to be seen more often in the late evening, although they are often all over the place just after dawn in late spring. It is appropriate to mention here that deer watching is an activity not normally associated with this kind of walking. It usually involves a lot of patient waiting, in a particular spot which deer are known to frequent.

Park by the Norwegian Stone in Glenmore, cross the road, and go through the caravan/camp site to the lake shore. There is a large, clean, attractive, very sandy, and extremely popular beach at this end of the loch, and it is an excellent place to observe *Homo Sapiens*, as people busily enjoy their holiday in, on, or about the water. The warmly golden granite sands provide a substitute sea-side for children of all ages, and the loch itself supports all sorts of quiet water sports -- no noisy power boats and no water skiing.

Follow the shore-line to the left, to the Alt Mor estuary, where the beach is often thronged with optimistic anglers hoping, usually in vain, to hook a trout or pike (there is often better fly fishing at the other end of the loch, in the big pool at the beginning of the Luineag).

The Alt Mor has created an obvious delta, and this area of beach has been added during the past fifty years or so. The actual entry point into the loch can be seen to vary from year to year, which is geology in action. To the layman it is about as exciting as watching paint dry.

Go to the foot bridge, upstream to the left, cross to the other bank, and follow the stream down to the shore again. There is a marked change of atmosphere here, and this part of the loch is a quiet, shallow and reedy bay that looks very 'pikey' to any fisherman. Follow the shore-line, at first by the water's edge, and then through the woodland to a point where a path goes steeply uphill to the left. This leads onto a forest road that goes round the back of the loch, and the open aspect to the west, over the loch, is a good place from which to view some wonderful sunsets. Go left along the road, and then left again, through the woodland to the stream. Cross the bridge, and follow the stream back to the ski-road.

This is a basic short short walk of about a mile, but there is a veritable maze of paths and tracks at this end of the loch, and it is fun to use the map and make up your own private routes. They can cover a seemingly endless variety of new woodland, old woodland, loch side, stream side, meadow land, scrub land and marsh land. There are opportunities here for observing almost every type of life, and subjects range from humans, arguably at the top of the animal kingdom, down to tiny wood mites, which are almost certainly near the bottom. Interesting woodland birds abound, and water fowl and plant life are abundant. Or just sit on a log and think: but do be wary of the wood ants -- they bite like mad!

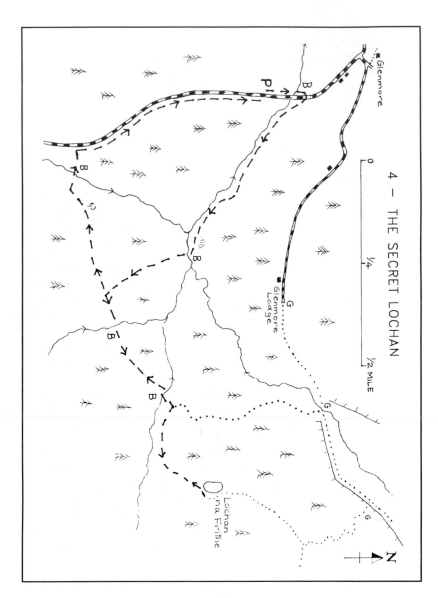

4 — THE SECRET LOCHAN

Glenmore

Glenmore Lodge

Lochan na Frithe

0   ¼   ½ MILE

N

4 -- THE SECRET LOCHAN IN THE FOREST.

The Queen's Forest is something of a hybrid, consisting, as it does, of a hard core of ancient woodland within a large area of new plantings. In this context, 'new' is relative, and much of the existing timber was planted in the immediately post-war years. It has now matured, and widespread felling is in progress here and there. Any one of the stacks of newly cut timber will provide an oppportunity for a ring count, and it takes only a few moments to see that most of the trees are about thirty years old, but the odd Scots pine log amongst the lumber will be very much older. This is a simple, yet vivid, illustration of the economic argument for the widespread planting of spruce, larch and fir.

The walk passes through much new woodland, and it should help to dispel the notion that all modern forestry is both ugly and sterile. Lochan na Frithe, literally the 'Lochan in the Forest', is one of the hidden delights of the the Queen's Forest. It is virtually 'on the door-step' for anybody staying in Glenmore, yet hardly anyone knows that it is there. This short walk of 2 miles is an ideal early evening stroll and that is the best time for it.

Park at the picnic area, that the Forestry Commission calls the Heron's field, at the start of the Wayfaring Course (NH980092). Walk back along the road for about 200 yards, cross over the bridge, and then take the forest road that strikes back alongside the burn. This is a picturesque stretch of water-side, and the view to the S is reminiscent of the Canadian Rockies. The Cairngorm corries, often snow-bedecked, loom large above the dense plantings of spruce, fir, larch and pine on the other side of the stream, where the extensive gravel strands provide nesting places for oyster catchers.

Just beyond the sheer and gritty face of an excavated drumlin ('sand-pit' seems so prosaic), the stream is bridged, and the path tends roughly S, through an area of dense forest. Then, in a recent clearing, at a 'T' junction with another forest road, the path is followed to the left. A Bailey bridge carries it over another stream and into more woodland. It crosses yet another area of roughly cleared ground, and there is a slight diversion to a crude bridge across a stream. Immediately after this a side road is followed, steeply uphill to the right, and through pleasantly varied new woodland. At last, as the gradient eases and the track bends to the left, the lochan is revealed, nestling in a green and reedy hollow.

Towards the end of the day, when the light is soft, when there is just a little wreath of mist, and when the blackish background conifers, silhouetted against the sky, are subtly back-lit by a low and rosy glowing sun, this is a most enchanting place. Listen to the silence of it all, and enjoy the peace and the quiet, alone in the forest with only deer and other wildlife for company. This is the stuff of pleasant dreams, and of imperishable memories.

If there seems to be something familiar about this place it may be that you have seen it on television. This is where the witch came by a lochan on a sledge in the adaptation of C.S. Lewis's Narnia fantasy of *The Lion, the Witch and the Wardrobe*.

Retrace the route, back over the Bailey bridge, but do not go right at the junction. Instead, go straight on along a wide and easy forest road through an area of old woodland. One tree, in a little glade on the right, commands attention: it is obviously of venerable age, and is so gnarled and twisted that it looks more like a greatly misplaced olive than a birch. Encrusted with moss, and festooned with lichens, in the twilight it could have been culled from a childish nightmare, and a few hob-goblins would not be out of place.

Further on, an arched timber bridge carries the path over the Allt Mor, and an absolute chaos of rocks, boulders and old tree debris is an eloquent testament to the volume, force and quite irresistible power of the melt waters that surge down from the hills from time to time. Normally there is very little water here, but the bridge is built high and wide to clear the stream that sometimes flows. Beyond the bridge the forest road changes to a sylvan path, and the sudden junction with the ski road can come as something of a shock. Go right for about 1/4 mile on the road-side verge, back to the start. Seasoned wayfarers and more adventurous walkers may care to try some of the possible alternative routes through the open rides, or along the smaller forest paths. Two are shown on the sketch map, but the official Wayfaring map provides a wealth of possibilities. See the Wayfaring Chapter.

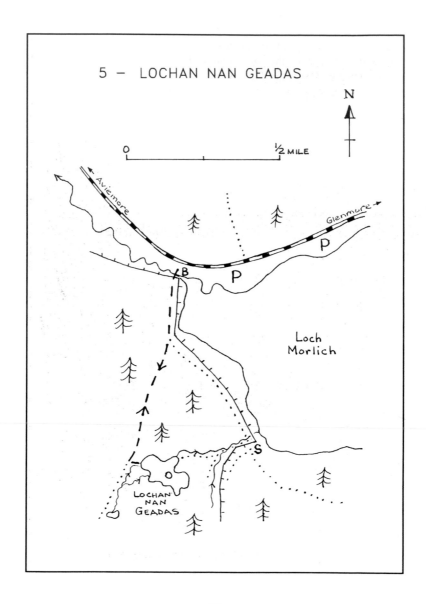

5 – LOCHAN NAN GEADAS

N

0 ½ MILE

Aviemore

Glenmore

B

P

P

Loch
Morlich

S

LOCHAN
NAN
GEADAS

LOCHAN nan GEADAS – Rothiemurchus

5 -- LOCHAN NAN GEADAS

Just up the road to Rothiemurchus Lodge, easily missed by the un-knowing, and overshadowed by Loch Morlich, its nearby big and famous neighbour, this little lochan has a charm and beauty of its own. It is a minor Mecca for knowledgeable bird-watchers, and one of its greatest charms is that it is impossible to forecast what will be there.

Cross the bridge at the W end of Loch Morlich (NH959096) and follow the track. At the point where the tracks divide, branch to the right, and after about 1/4 mile, just before a flooded gravel pit, look for a break in the young trees to the left. The lochan is fed by a little stream, and is well hidden. There is a very pleasant resting place beneath the branches of a venerable old Scots pine, round to

Wildcat

the left from the approach path, and it makes a most convenient natural hide from which to watch the comings and goings of the birds. The avian population varies with the day, not just with the season, and the following are typical: goosander (nest boxes, like upended coffins, on the island), widgeon, oyster catcher and goldeneye. There is, of course, no guarantee that any particular birds, or even any birds, will be seen during any given visit, but the chances are that one will be pleasantly surprised, and the lochan is worth visiting just for its own sake. There is no such thing as a wasted day when out and about here.

. This location is included with some misgivings because it is one of the author's favourite places, and it would be a shame to see a good thing ruined by the pressures of too many people. So if you should arrive and find that another has beaten you to it, then go away until some other time. Better by far to leave it for another day, rather than force the wildfowl to leave it for ever.

Crossbill

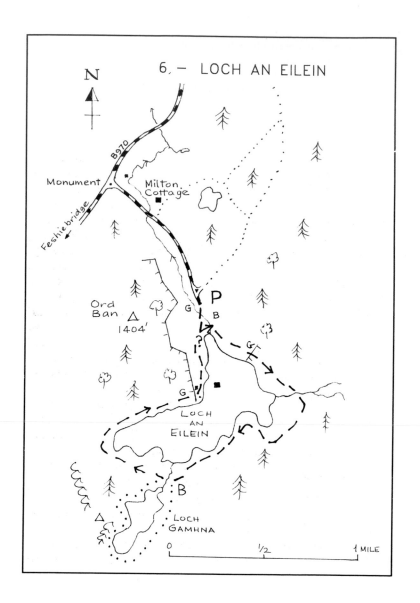

6. – LOCH AN EILEIN

N

B970

Monument

Feshiebridge

Milton
Cottage

Ord
Ban △
1404'

G P B

G

G

Loch
an
Eilein

G

B

△

Loch
Gamhna

0   ½   1 MILE

6:-- LOCH AN EILEIN

Loch an Eilean has nearly everything: in an idyllic setting in an ancient woodland, it is backed by dramatic crags. It has a varied and most attractive shoreline, and a romantic ruined castle on an island. It is possible to drive there from both N and S on good if somewhat narrow roads, and it is also possible to walk there almost entirely on footpaths. There is a large car park, a Visitor Centre, a toilet block, and a nature trail on adequate but not overdone paths. One could go on and on, but, in a nutshell, Loch an Eilein has virtually all that the casual tripper could desire. Despite this, and notwithstanding its consequent popularity, it remains an extraordinarily pleasant place.

The loch lies in the largest surviving fragment of the old Caledonian Forest, and here, in Rothiemurchus, there is a most varied and interesting range of wildlife to be seen by the experienced and careful observer. The casual visitor is unlikely to see much of the larger animals, but roe deer and red squirrels are not uncommon, and there are always plenty of butterflies, birds, and interesting plants. A short walk around the loch is, perhaps, a perfect introduction to Rothiemurchus forest. It is always an enjoyable experience, and it is a good alternative to the hills if the clouds are down, or if it it is too hot to be away from shade.

Across the way from the Ranger Centre at Inverdruie (NH901110)) a minor road goes roughly SE. After about a mile, by the Martineau memorial, there is a branch road to the left that goes down to the car park by the loch (NH98086). The route is signposted.

Some time spent in the Visitor Centre, **before** going anywhere else, will greatly increase the pleasure of a walk here. Then take the track to the left for a clockwise circuit of the loch. At the N end of the loch the land is relatively open, and this shore can offer good views of the ruin, which is close enough for photographs, but not so close that it dominates the view. This little castle is reputed to have been a 14/15th century stronghold of one Alexander Stewart, the legendary Wolf of Bad- enoch, a local warlord and a notorious bandit. A bastard son of the Scottish King Bruce II, he was infamous for having sacked and burned the cathedral of Elgin. The castle is also known to have been the last refuge of the osprey until it was finally harried out of existence as a British nesting species about the turn of the century. The birds have had the last laugh. Their numbers have grown since their re-introduction at Loch Garten in the 1950's, and ospreys now fish the loch again. Some also nest in the locality, and they spend the summer in Rothiemurchus. Crested tits and crossbills are less spectacular birds that also nest here, but they are also rarities, and may be of equal interest to keen birdwatchers.

Birds are only one aspect of the very varied wildlife to be seen in the vicinity, and there are botanical surprises, too. For example, the yellow figwort is a plant that has really no business to be here at all: supposedly found mainly in southern England, a very healthy specimen was in flower in a crevice in a wall by the Visitor Centre not all that long ago. There are many fungi in the birch thickets on the W side of the loch, and one of the bracket fungi -- *fomes fomentarius* --occurs in only one other locality in Britain. It was avidly collected many years ago because the dried and shredded flesh was ideal kindling in a tinder box, and there was also a short-lived Victorian vogue for drawings executed on the parchment-like surface of the gills.

The ruined buildings around the Visitor Centre are all that remains of a timber industry that flourished here in the 18th century, and many of the older trees date from around that time. They may be found at the southern end of the loch, and some of them would have been seedlings at the time of the 1745 rebellion led by Prince Charles Edward Stewart, the Bonny Prince Charlie of legend.

It is possible to make a diversion at the S end of the loch and stroll around little Loch Gamhna. It is also a glacial loch, but must be at a very late stage in its development because it is now very shallow and it has a totally different character from its relative next door. Separated by only a few yards in distance, they are worlds apart in atmosphere and appearance. The water lillies are a picture.

The whole of the Loch an Eilein reserve is included in the National Nature Reserve by agreement with the Rothiemurchus Estate, and visitors have access to the network of private paths and rights of way that criss-cross the forest of Rothiemurchus. It is an enchanting place, and is totally unlike the common concept of a conifer forest. This sylvan wilderness is a place of great beauty, and it is sanctuary for many species that are rare or extinct elsewhere. It is a primeval paradise that can occupy and entertain the artist, naturalist, photographer, or mere wanderer, for a very long time.

WOLF'S LAIR — LOCH AN EILEIN

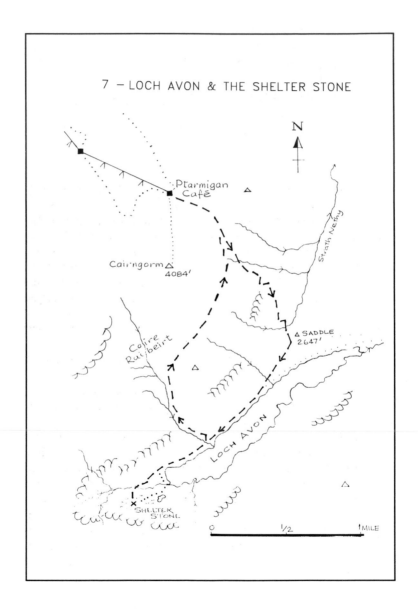

7 — LOCH AVON & THE SHELTER STONE

N

Ptarmigan
Café

Cairngorm
4084'

Strath Nethy

△ SADDLE
2647'

Coire
Raibeirt

LOCH AVON

SHELTER
STONE

0   1/2   1 MILE

7-- LOCH AVON AND THE SHELTER STONE

Loch Avon has the distinction of being the highest large lake in Britain, and prior to the installation of the Cairngorm ski-lift it was very hard to get to. Most visitors to the great plateau are probably quite unaware of its existence, since it cannot be seen at all from the summit of Cairngorm, and a fair walk is needed to get even a glimpse of the water. The loch lies at the head of the Loch Avon Trench, a great blind canyon that slashes through the mountains from the east. It is a spectacular relic of the glaciations that have played the major part in the shaping of this wild and very beautiful countryside, and it is probably little changed since the end of the last Ice Age.

Perhaps the greatest attraction of this place for the normal hill walker is its remote and unspoilt beauty. For the rock climber it is just Paradise, with a myriad routes, of every grade, on the fissured and fractured granite crags that rise for hundreds of feet above the sandy shore at the head of the loch.

At the foot of the soaring cliffs there is a crazy jumble of giant stones and boulders, brought down from above by the endless attrition of the frost and ice. In the midst of this stony chaos, one ancient granite block, about the size of a small house and weighing some 1300 tons, has formed a natural refuge somewhat like a gigantic dolmen. It is unmistakable, and is the famous 'Shelter Stone'. It is often referred to as a bothy, but that is stretching things a mite too far. However, it can provide shelter for several people for a bivouac on a balmy summer's night. It was the birthplace of The

Cairngorm Club, the oldest climbing club in Scotland (read *Mountain Days and Bothy Nights*), and it really is unusual and very picturesque. It is also the objective for this short walk, and the round trip on a fine day will provide a fairly energetic and very memorable outing.

From the top station of the chairlift do not go up to Cairngorm summit. Instead follow the fenced track to the left and make for the top of the ridge, then zig-zag downhill to the right, going roughly SE. The way down is not very obvious, and there is no path, but common sense will direct the walker away from the large rock outcrops. There are a couple of streams to cross, with a great rock face to the right. Aim to pass below this, and there will soon be a choice of several deer tracks all heading down towards the Saddle.

The Saddle marks the watershed between the rivers Avon and Nethy, and is in an idyllic setting. The scenery in all directions is unforgettable. In particular, the view along Loch Avon towards Shelter Stone Crag is indescribably beautiful. Strath Nethy lies behind, and provides the bad weather 'escape route' from the area. Upper Glen Avon opens out to the left, and separates the mountain masses of A'Choinneach and Beinn Mheadhoin as it cradles the infant river at the start of its journey to the Spey. Ahead, mirrored on the pellucid water of the loch, a great amphitheatre of mighty crags dominates the view. This is an awesome wall of rugged granite, white veined and criss-crossed by the many streams cascading down from the great plateau below Ben MacDui. The head walls are usually also patched with snow, and beneath Ben MacDui summit a great snowfield can be seen, which often lies there the year round.

From the Saddle, a narrow track on the right goes gently down towards the Loch, some 300 feet below. During this descent, a burn is crossed immediately below the great rock wall of Stac an Fharaidh. The way undulates, sometimes up and sometimes down, but always stony and always full of interest. After about a mile, another much larger stream comes roaring and cascading down the hill. It can always be forded, but the best spot to cross may be a little way off the path. Notice the faint track going uphill on the right side of this burn: this is the way up to Coire Raibeirt, and is the return route to Cairngorm. The shore-side track is followed to the head of the loch, where a delightful beach of pink granite sand makes a vivid contrast with the deep blue water. It looks an ideal place to bathe, and is very tempting on a hot day. Be advised that the water is very deep and is always icy cold, and be content with a paddle in the shallows! Climb the hillock behind the shore, and look for the Shelter Stone at the foot of its eponymous crag. It is easily identified. To get there, it is necessary to cross the stream flowing into the loch. Boots off, and it is easily forded near its entry to the loch. The fords are marked on the 1:25000 OS map.

Once beneath the Shelter Stone it will take a little time to become accustomed to the gloom. It is clear that eight or ten people can stretch out here with a degree of comfort, but it is certainly not 'Five Star' accommodation, and there is no incentive to linger. Cross the stream again, and follow the shore track back to the Coire Raibeirt burn. The way goes straight up on the right-hand side, and it

PTARMIGAN

is steep and strenuous climbing for some 600 feet. Calling for hands as well as feet in many places, some of the going is an easy and exhilarating scramble on the water-splashed granite. There will be mixed feelings as the steep ascent eases off into the gentle undulations of Coire Raibeirt. Achievement, elation, and sheer wonder will all be mixed with a feeling of exhaustion. The exhaustion will soon pass: the sense of achievement and the wonder will long remain.

This is a marvellous vantage point from which to view the hill country to the south, across Loch Etchachan and Derry Cairngorm. The prospect is a revelation, and a delight that never palls. Keep going over the soggy tundra, heading uphill, making roughly NE, and contouring to the right round the base of Cairngorm summit back to the chairlift. Remember that the last chair down is about 4pm in summer, and plan the day accordingly. This is a short but strenuous walk of about 5 miles, and at least six hours need to be allowed if it is to be unhurried.

SHELTER STONE - Loch Avon

THE MOUNTAINS

The Roman general Agricola beat the Picts at the battle of Mons Graupus in 84AD. The exact location of Mons Graupus is unknown. A Scottish historian, Hector Boece, working in Dundee at the start of the 16th century used Tacitus's account of the battle, but he misread the name as Graupus, and that is how the Grampians were named: by accident, just a fortuitous slip of the pen.

The Grampians lie between the Highland Boundary Fault and the Great Glen, a quite arbitrary division which covers an enormous area and includes a complex mixture of mountain groups that differ greatly in appearance, constitution, character and age. They have virtually only one thing in common, and that is their involvement in the last ice-age. The Cairngorms are ancient mountains, and they stand higher than their surroundings because the granite of which they are made is harder than the rocks of the adjoining hills. All these central highlands are the ground-down remnants of much higher mountains created an unimaginably long time ago. The great, Everest-like peaks have gone, worn away by incessant weathering, and here, in the east, a vast and undulating table-land remains, and most of the highest ground was apparently untouched by the last glaciation.

The predominant mountain-building activity of the Caledonian period left its mark in the uniform SW/NE alignments of such features as the Great Glen, and the Findhorn and Spey river valleys. There are other deeply etched features which do not conform, and obvious local examples are the Lairig Ghru, the Loch Avon Trench and Glen Garry. In all these cases, the natural grain and lie of the land have been emphasised and exaggerated by the sculpting action of moving ice, which has also produced such dramatic features as the great corries on the N face of Cairngorm.

Glen Garry sweeps round in a great arc from Perth, through Blair Atholl and up to Drumochter summit. The pass then changes its direction and runs down to Newtonmore, where it opens out a little as it spreads and merges into the valley of the Spey. It provides an artery for road and rail as it slices through the mountains, and it neatly separates the Cairngorms and the Monadhliaths. The physical beauty of the country, its climate, and the ease of access, coupled with increased leisure and good publicity, have made this one of the most rapidly developing playgrounds in Britain. Once the preserve of only the most hardy mountaineers and naturalists, the Cairngorms now attract tens of thousands of visitors, and they come at all times of the year.

Easy access can bring problems, and it must be realised that, in general, this is not a region where the new or inexperienced fell-walker can wander at will with impunity. Walkers on the Cairngorm plateau need to acquire a fair degree of high-level wisdom, and they need to know their limitations on both the good days and the bad. In this context, 'high-level' refers to altitude, not to intellect. It is wise to measure mountain walks in hours, not in miles, and there are very good reasons for the distinction. The Cairngorm plateau is not a place where one can ignore, or be blasé about the climate. Unlike the mountains in the rest of Britain, this is an area of sub-arctic tundra, and the winter weather here can be as severe as that experienced anywhere else in the world. There are snow fields that lie all the year round, and it is not at all unusual to have the odd quick blizzard in mid-summer. The great mountain fastness of the Cairngorm massif is still a wild, desolate and remote country; it is a barren wilderness with the most extreme climate in Britain, and it has a savage but attractive beauty that grips one and doesn't let go.

There is much good walking, too, on the adjacent smaller hills,

Roe buck

and several of the following walks are based on these. They offer some of the most impressive viewpoints in the Cairngorms, and they can provide delightful walking away from the crowds.

-44-

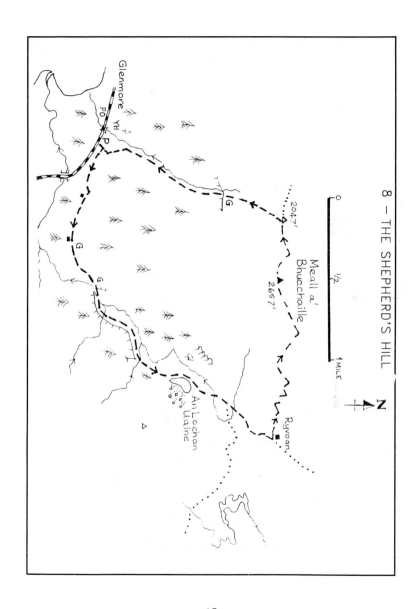

8 – THE SHEPHERD'S HILL

N

0 ½ 1 MILE

Glenmore

YH

PO

P

G

G

G

2047'

Meall a'
Bhuachaille

2657'

Ryvoan

An Lochan
Uaine

8 -- SHEPHERD'S HILL

The Kincardines form the northern boundary of Glen More, and the long ridge runs from behind Kincardine Chapel to Ryvoan, where it ends in the prominent lump of Meall a' Bhuachaille, which, in English, means The Shepherd's Hill. In the context of the adjacent Cairngorms it is a mere pimple, but at 2654 feet it is a considerable hill in its own right, and it is tailor-made for an energetic short hill-walk.

Start from the little car park in Glenmore, and follow the directions for Walk 1 as far as An Lochan Uaine. From the lochan, continue along the stony track, and ignore the branch to the right, which leads to Strath Nethy and the Lairig an Laoigh (The Pass of the Calves). Keep straight on to where, at the top of the rise, a red-roofed stone building is set in a large area of rough grassland. This is Ryvoan, a fine example of one of the classic bothies, and it is still well cared for outside. Inside there is Spartan, but no doubt welcome, accommodation for a wild and stormy night. There used to be a Visitors Book, which made interesting and amusing reading, but the writing of obscenities and other apparently moronic malpractices have resulted in its removal during the summer months. What a sad commentary on our times, and on some of the people who now come here.

Immediately outside the door a well marked track heads roughly NW, straight up the hill. During the climb do pause from time to time and look back. A lovely panorama gradually unfolds and the ground below, which at bothy level seems to be just rough scrub and heather, is seen to be an undulating country of glacial debris, with numerous ravines, streams and little lochans. Beyond Loch

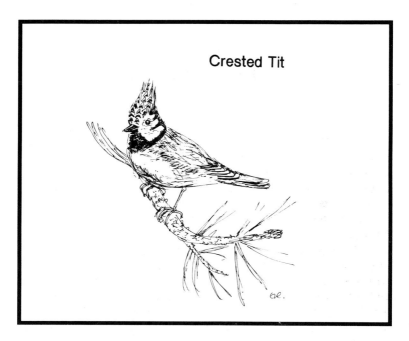

Crested Tit

a'Gharbh Choire, the mouth of Strath Nethy starts to open up between Mam Suim and An Lurg, and the Lairig an Laoigh can be seen snaking up the distant hill before it passes behind the whale-back Bynack Ridge.

There is a short but steep section that may require the use of hands as well as feet, but the gradient soon eases and it is then an easy walk to the summit.

From the hill top, there is, on a fine day with good visibility, a superb and extensive view, and a large cairn provides adequate protection from the wind. Abernethy Forest and Loch Garten lie broadly to the N, with the Lochindorb moors in the distance beyond, whilst to the NW the whole of Strath Spey is displayed. Looking W, there are the Monadhliaths, and coming round to the SW, Loch Alvie and Loch an Eilein lie beyond the broad sweep of Rothiemurchus

Forest, where Carn Eilrig stands alone, guarding the ways into Glen Einich and the Lairig Ghru. To the S, and immediately below, Loch Morlich sparkles like a sapphire in the warm sunshine, as it nestles in the dark emerald cushion of the Queen's Forest. The Cairngorm massif dominates the view to the SW, and provides a dramatic backdrop with its distant prospect of the great corries. Finally, away to the E across the Nethy, the great ridge of the Bynacks looks exactly like a petrified prehistoric beast.

An obvious path strikes downhill from the summit, and at the col there is a cairn and a parting of the ways. The track to the right goes up to Creagan Gorm, and, eventually, to the end of the ridge. It is an old stalking road, and there is plenty of evidence of the continued presence of grouse and deer. The way down is by the track to the left, which is followed through grassland, stiff with cloudberries at first, and then increasingly wooded, and then by a gentle and very pleasant stream. It can be a bit boggy towards the bottom of the hill, and the best way is not always obvious. Eventually, the grass gives way to a forest road which leads to Glenmore. This is a moderately strenuous walk of about five miles, and it provides a quite delightful change away from the hordes on Cairngorm.

9 — CASTLE HILL

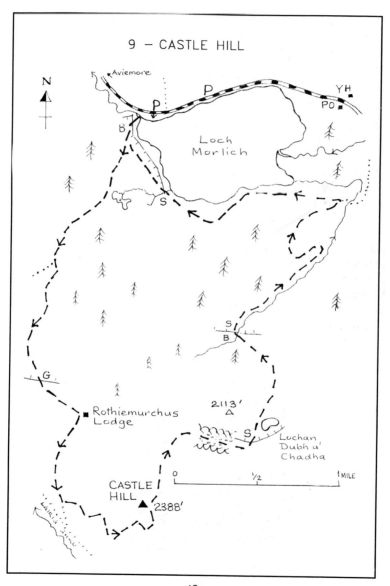

9 -- CASTLE HILL

Some hills give a very good return for the effort necessary to climb them. Carn Eilrig is, perhaps, the supreme example in this area, but, in the compass of this book, it is out of bounds, mainly because it is too far away. Castle Hill is much more accessible, and the summit views are almost as good.

Park in the picnic area by the Bailey Bridge at the foot of Loch Morlich (NH958096). Cross the bridge and walk up the track towards the Lodge. The surface has been much improved in recent years, and a recent topping of hard-rolled granite grit has resulted in a surface that is quite good to walk on. Pray that it will not be tar-macadamed in the future! Ignore the track to the right to Piccadilly and keep on, past the Lodge, and down towards the Lairig Ghru. Castle Hill is the hillside on the left.

Shortly before the track meets the Lairig Ghru, start to climb the hillside to the left. There is no particular point to start the climb, and no particular route: just try to find the clearest ground, and avoid, as far as possible, the occasional boulder fields. The idea is to zig-zag up the hill, tending slightly left, to gain the 2370 feet lower summit cairn. At about 2000 feet there is a lonely and surprisingly large silver birch. Don't search for it, and don't worry if it isn't there: all ways up lead to the top!

The steepish hillside eases off to a small and flattish top. It is a mixture of wire grass, lichens, and mosses, and has a pleasant springy texture like a dry loofah. It is very good to walk on. A small cairn gives some shelter from the wind, and the top itself provides an ideal platform from which to view a vast and varied tract of countryside. The panorama encompasses the Lairig up to the E flank of Cairn Toul, the woodlands of Rothiemurchus, the N face of the Cairngorm ridge, and the country over towards the Kincardines and Glen More. Across the Lairig Ghru, the view to the SE is dominated by Sron na Lairige and the immense bulk of Braeriach. The W foreground is largely occupied by the Lairig Ghru, backed by Carn Eilrig, and this is a good spot from which to watch deer in the calving grounds around the upper limit of the trees. The presence of large numbers of calving hinds is one reason for avoiding that hill in late spring and early summer. Later on there may be deer stalking.

Deer also frequent Castle Hill, and they sometimes use the nick between the N and S summits as a passage to the Lochain bowl. A cast antler has been found on the hill as late as the end of May.

Across the valley to the NE is the lowly eminence of Silver Hill. Start down towards this, but ensure that the route strays only slightly to the E of N. This direction leads down the W of the glacial overflow channel of Eag a'Chait -- Cat's Notch. This little canyon is delightfully sheltered and secluded, and many rowans grow in the sun-splashed pockets betwen the rocks. Pick up the track from Rothiemurchus Lodge and go through the notch. There is a little boulder field which requires some care, but the track is plain. Once through the notch, climb gently to the left, up to the fence of the reindeer compound. There is a stile, which should be crossed, and the track is then followed past Lochan Dubh Chada and down into the forest.

By a woodman's hut the rough track meets a forest road where a crude sign, nailed to a tree, warns: **'Rangifer Tarrandus! Beware of the Bulls!'** It refers, of course, to reindeer, and the way leads off down the road to the right. There are many mature trees and much timber extraction in this area, and it is interesting and pleasing to note that the native Scots pines are usually left standing when the alien conifers are clear-felled. At the next junction go to the left, and follow the forest road back to the starting point.

10 – CREAG NAN GALL

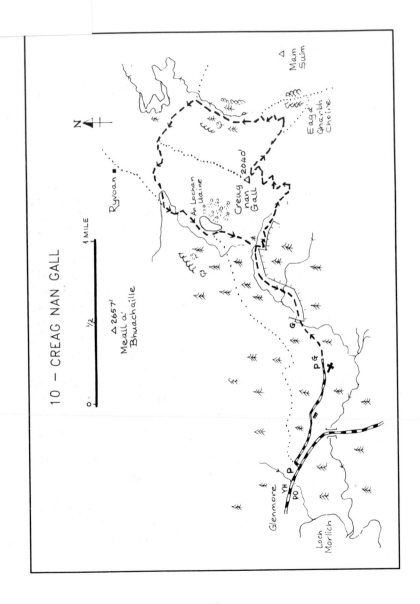

10 -- CREAG NAN GALL -- STRANGER'S HILL

All travellers through the Ryvoan Pass are aware of Creag nan Gall. Its impressive, steep and stony tree-clad face rises staight up from the waters of Lochan Uaine. The scree-clad slope is so steep it is obvious that it cannot be climbed directly, but the Creag can be got at from behind.

Park in the little lay-by near the gate just beyond new Glenmore Lodge (NH987095) AND PLEASE DO NOT OBSTRUCT THE GATE WAY. Follow the Ryvoan track through Glen More to where a forest fence, on the right, goes off sharply up the hill a little way short of Lochan Uaine. A fairly well-worn track roughly parallels the fence. This is part of one of the Forestry Commission's forest walks, and there are likely to be marker posts. Ignore any arrows pointing down. Follow this track to where it levels off on a fairly open moorland which stretches away to the right. At this point bear left over a little ridge, and down to where a small and stony stream waters a few small trees at the foot of the hill. This quiet and secluded little glade is typical of the many secret sun traps to be found around the fringes of the Caingorm hills.

Follow the narrow track, which contours the hillside a little way above the stream, and goes in the general direction of Cairngorm N ridge. After a few hundred yards, just about the point where a wooded gorge on the moor appears far away to the right, the deep heather of the hillside gives way to a steep, narrow, stony, but grassy slope to the left. There appears to be a track of sorts, and it is possibly a deer stalkers' way up this unfrequented hill. Follow this track, and when it peters out, as it surely will, seek out the more open ground whilst zig-zagging up to the left. The ridge will soon appear, and it is then an easy stroll to the summit across a carpet of firm and springy turf.

This airy hill top provides a breath-taking panorama of the country to the north, and a short walk downhill provides a bird's eye view of Loch a'Gharbh Choire, which dominates the foreground. The eye ranges over Abernethy, and then carries on until the horizon blues and merges with the sky in the far distance.

Eastwards, and round to the south, the long views are blocked by the bulk of Cairngorm's N ridge, but the lack of distance is well compensated by a wealth of interest. The glacial nature of the terrain is quite evident, and a possible ancient lake shore at about 1800 feet is reminiscent of the parallel roads of Glen Roy. From this vantage point, it looks like a Land Rover track but it isn't. It is a pretty good route up to the summit ridge. The steep and craggy face that overlooks the Green Lochan is a short walk downhill to the W, and the view from the edge is really spectacular. It is not recommended to sufferers from vertigo!

There is a choice of return routes from the summit, depending on how short this particular walk needs to be. The easy option is to simply walk down to the N. The springy hill-top turf gives way to deep heather, and the hill side is stony and in places damp, but the slope is gentle. This way leads down to the Laraig an Laioigh track near the Ryvoan junction. A slightly longer, but much more interesting return may be made by An Gharbh Choire, which runs in from the N, over towards Mam Suim. For this route, follow the obvious track to the E, and where the track goes downhill to circumvent the Eag, go off to the left, and carefully descend the peaty and grassy slope into the corrie. It is steep but easy, and the rewards of this longer route are very great. This delectable small valley is one of the treasures of the district, and is a place of endless delights. The little crags, the rowan-garlanded rock faces, a tiny lochan, a trout stream, and a few venerable pines combine to enrich a secret place that lingers in the memory.

Follow the path to the main track, and go left for Glenmore.

CAIRNGORM

Not the least important feature of this mountain is its sheer accessibility. The first chairlift was erected in 1961, but even before that, Cairngorm was the most easily approached of the 4000 feet summits of the Cairngorm hills. True, it is some nine miles from Aviemore, but there has long been a road of sorts to Glenmore Lodge, and a track beyond there. The favoured way was up the windy ridge of An t'Aonach, and the track may still be found just above Clach Bharraig, the Foundation Stone, an enormous erratic boulder, prominent on the hillside to the left, just before the road straightens up to run into the main carpark. For anyone disposed to walk up or down the hill, this is probably a better route than the dreary toil on the track beside the chairlift towers.

Seen from a reasonable distance, say a mile or so, the N face of Cairngorm is an impressive sight. Close-to, it is a right mess in places, and Coire Cas is an awful mixture of eroded hillside, snow fences, a weird collection of assorted ironmongery, and a service road. It doesn't look bad in winter, and early spring, when snow provides a blanket to hide the wounds, and a multitude of skiers obscures the multitude of devices used to get them up the hill, but the skiing season is short, and for the rest of the year the flank of the mountain in Coire Cas is a sorry sight. Here, with a vengeance, is vivid proof that distance lends enchantment to the view.

In the context of the mountain the disfigurement is very small, and the Chairlift Company do all they can to mitigate the effects of tens of thousands of visitors. This includes a lot of landscape repair work, and we are all part of the problem. The company are bogeymen to the conservationists because of their proposal to site ski tows in Lurchers Meadow. One can have some sympathy with both sides, but if it went ahead, and was an ecological disaster, it could not be undone. Perhaps the pressure will subside a little now that more ski grounds have been developed on Ben Nevis.

SHELTER STONE CRAG – from Cairngorm

11 – 13 CAIRNGORM WALKS

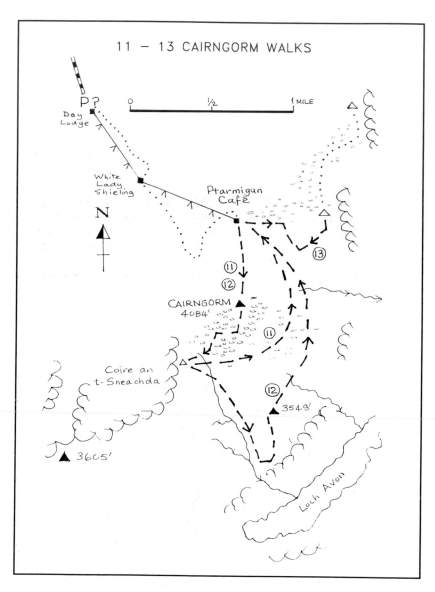

11 -- THE DUKE OF YORK'S MARCH

'The grand old Duke of York, he had ten thousand men, he marched them up to the top of the hill, and he marched them down again....'

Thus goes the old nursery rhyme, and thus it would seem, go most of the 1000 people who, on average, ride up Cairngorm on the chairlift virtually every day of the year. And why not? Apart from Snowdon, which can be ascended by rack-railway, Cairngorm is the most easily ascended high mountain in Britain.

BLUE HARE

Book a return, and take the chairlift to the top station, which is at 3600 feet. After the ride, a relatively easy ascent of 500 feet on carefully graded granite slabs leads to the summit at 4084 feet. Westwards, the view passes over the great corries, with their sheer cliffs and lingering snow, then ranges across Loch Morlich to Rothiemurchus, the Monadhliaths, and beyond. The Spey valley opens towards the N from distant Aviemore, and the moors beyond Abernethy stretch away from the foreground bulk of the Kincardine Hills. Eastwards, the view encompasses the Bynacks, and across the Loch Avon trench -- invisible from here because of the contour of the hill -- the granite-torred Ben Avon massif lies behind the knobbly foreground bulk of Beinn Mheadhoin. To the S, little Loch Etchachan nestles in the cradle of its surrounding peaks. To the right of the loch the great hump of Ben MacDui dominates the view, and right again from that, the summits of Cairn Toul, Angels Peak and Braeriach all pop up from the far side of the Lairig Ghru. Whatever the season, there will be snowfields somewhere in view, and the essentially sub-arctic nature of the terrain is clear for all to see. It will be notably cooler than down below.

When seen from the N, which is the aspect open to the roads, the range is steep and craggy, and is mountainous indeed. The new visitor may then be surprised by the prospect S from the summit of Cairngorm. There **are** craggy mountains to be seen from here, but they are all quite far away, and the immediate surroundings are more akin to rolling moorland, which is exactly what the Cairngorm plateau is, but because of its altitude and climate, it is in fact tundra, and very interesting to the naturalist. It will be quite evident that little in the way of normal vegetation exists on the summit, and the ground cover is mainly rough and scarified granite grit bestrewn with sundry boulders. There are patches of vegetation here and there, but they are very sparse and frugal, and there is little or no grass. There are just irregular and somewhat crusty cakes, which consist mainly of sedges, club mosses and lichens. This is a barren wilderness indeed, and it is an uncomfortable place on a cold grey day with a chill wind. Most people who come this far have a look at the weather station and the views, take a few photographs and then go down the way they came up. That is fine, so far as it goes, but Cairngorm has more than that to offer to the interested visitor.

Follow the faint track down to the west that goes towards the edge of Sneachda corrie. Then leave the hordes, bear off left, and contour round the base of the hill. There is a marked change in vegetation here, and a sparse grass appears, with some trifid rush poking through in the damp patches. Sundry small clumps of moss campion are dotted about, and its pink flowers add a welcome touch of warm colour in early summer. The study of the lichens and mosses could be a life's work in itself, but very little effort is needed to experience their variety and beauty close-to. In pride of place, perhaps, are the grey-green cladonias with their bright red fruiting bodies, and there is a most picturesque brimstone-yellow patchy lichen which favours quartz blocks, and grows in company with another lichen, which is sooty black. They produce very attractive and photogenic patterns on the rocks. It is pleasant and comfortable walking, and as the way bends round again towards the N, the ground rises and ski tows come into view, disused and abandoned until the winter. Go downhill now, back to the chairlift.

12 -- COIRE RAIBEIRT AND STAC AN FHARAIDH

Climb to Cairngorm summit from the top station of the chairlift, descend towards Coire an t-Sneachda and walk over to the cairn, as for the previous walk, then turn left and go gently downhill into Coire Raibeirt. This is a gathering ground for snow melt water, and an appreciable stream may be followed over an area of peculiar wetland. The ground is soggy but quite firm, and there is only a very thin crust of wet vegetation on the underlying rock. Much of the moss is black, which seems to be typical of mosses that spend much of each year beneath the snow cover. As the slope increases, cross over to the left and make for the cliff top, following the faint track that ascends from Loch Avon. This position provides a good viewpoint for the massive cliffs at the head of the loch, and it also gives a view of the loch and of the Shelter Stone.

Turn left again, and follow the edge up to the rocky eminence of Stac an Fharaidh. There are some dramatic views from up here, and the S prospect is practically as good as that from Cairngorm summit, with the added bonus of a sight of Loch Avon immediately and far below.

Turn back from the summit of the Stac, and carry on contouring round the base of the hill to the N. The grassy tundra here is home to many ptarmigan, and there is always the chance of an eagle over the loch. When the ski tows appear over the crest of the rise, bear left, and then go downhill to the chairlift.

This quiet and gentle walk of three to four miles needs about as many hours if it is to be enjoyed to the full.

13 -- CNAP COIRE NA SPREIDHE

Hardly a hill walk, this gentle stroll on the undulating plateau to the N of Cairngorm is quite undemanding. It is the thing to do on a roasting hot day when a quiet picnic is all that is required, well away from the crowds, but in the sun.

On leaving the chairlift, go past the Ptarmigan cafe and follow the fenced way to the left -- there may be a skiers signpost to Aonaich, etc. When the rise is breasted, bear left and make for the very obvious large tor, about a quarter of a mile away and a little to the right. The way is over a gently undulating moorland of springy

SNIPE

turf with, here and there, exposed slabs of weathered granite.

Close-to, the tor will be a surprise, being much larger than imagined from a first sight at a distance. It is a very large lump of weathered granite, rising from a clutter of long detached slabs and boulders at the summit of a small swelling on the face of the surrounding plateau. How it has survived the onslaught of aeons of weathering is a mystery, but it *has* survived, and this, and its fellows, are something of a local feature, as can be seen from the adjacent ridges of Beinn Mheadhoin and the Bynacks. No smooth and water-worn rock faces here; the tor is cracked and jointed, its surface is extremely rough, and its generally beat-up and well-worn appearance is a testament to the weathering of the last umpteen million years. It is eminently climbable, and the view from the little table top of its summit is well worth the effort of getting there.

On a fine and clear day there will be a strong temptation to carry on walking, it is so very pleasant. Do not resist the urge: there is another tor not far away, and the rocky edge of Sron a'Cha No offers dramatic views of Srath Nethy, and the red corrie of Bynack Beag. The way back is obvious.

GLEN FESHIE

This little-visited gem, which runs down the western margin of the Cairngorms, is one of Scotland's loveliest glens. There is a slow transition from the bleak and hostile tundra of Britain's highest mountain plateau to the soft and verdant pastures by the riverside. Typical of the Grampians, the landscape bears the unmistakeable stamp of its glacial past, but there is a marked contrast between this most delightful of river valleys, which provides a lonely but lovely walking route from Kingussie to Braemar, and those other N-S routes, the Lairig an Laoigh and the Lairig Ghru. A broad strath of the softest green is dotted here and there with the brown and ochre mounds of ancient drumlins. Nicely rounded hills, with rocky scars and outcrops, provide a dramatic back-drop for the trees. Gnarled and knotted old Scots pines alternate with weeping birch and prickly junipers, and the river is always close at hand. In places there may be up to a dozen separate streams, and little lawns of lush green grass provide ideal picnic spots between the rills of icy water draining down from An Moine Mhor -- the Great Moss.

English visitors who know the Lakes will feel very much at home, because there is a very 'Lakeland' feel about it all, but the resemblance ends with that. There is a marked lack of tourist hordes, and a very different scale: Glen Feshie is simply vast. It provides plenty of space and plenty of scope for artists, walkers, naturalists, botanists, birdwatchers and sundry other discerning folk. Seekers after solitude, they can all find here something very special in the peace and quiet, and in the absence of the frenzied activity that is now so apparent in many other parts of the Cairngorms. About ten miles above Feshiebridge there is a confluence of several streams, and the Feshie turns sharply up towards the east. The valley walls pull sharply in, and the valley floor begins to climb towards the watershed. This is reached at about 1800 feet, where Glen Feshie merges into Mar and meets the headwaters of the Geldie Burn.

Other than the long way round via Tomintoul, this is the only easy passage between Speyside and Deeside. From time to time there have been proposals for a road through the glen, and the route was first surveyed by General Wade in the 18th century. More recent was a survey in the 1950's, but high cost and low usage probably mean that the glen will be left alone, and will long remain a haven for those seeking a particular kind of peace.

The wilderness is more apparent than real, and there was much activity here in the past. The glen has been lived in since early times, and one authority derived the name from Feshor Fora, a 10th century Pictish chief. There are the remains of several farms, and there once was a thriving timber industry. Most of the old pines of Caledon were felled during World War I, but some well thought-out schemes of re-afforestation are putting matters right. There are still many areas of pleasant mature woodland, with a mixture of both coniferous and broad-leaved trees, and the glen is famous for its deer -- it is not uncommon to see herds of several hundred moving on the hill.

It is important to remember that deer stalking goes on here in the appropriate season. Between 15th August and 31st January walkers should not go on the hills here without first talking to the Stalker. He can be found at Carnachuin, by the Monument (NN845939), a little to the north of Feshie Lodge.

Access can be something of a problem. It is not a matter of getting onto the land -- that is easy -- it is the sheer difficulty of getting there at all. The good walking starts about 5 miles south of Feshiebridge, and that is at least 10 miles from both Aviemore and Kingussie.

There are various options: small parties (not more than three people) might be given permission to drive down to Glenfeshie Lodge. Phone the day before, and, if permission is granted, the gate key can be collected from the Suie Hotel. The preferred alternative is to drive down the road on the other side of the river to Achlean, where a car can be parked in a little lay-by above, and just before, the farm (NN852976). Larger groups can hire a minibus with driver, to deliver and collect at given times. This can be a very economic form of travel, and ten people can do the combined round trip from Aviemore for about £3 per head. Try Bill's Taxis, Aviemore 811105.

Whatever the effort, whatever the time and trouble involved in getting there, one thing is certain: it will be well worthwhile. Glen Feshie is a rarity that beckons one to return time and time again.

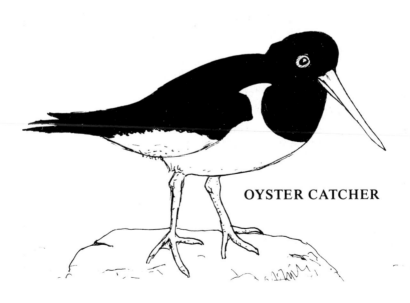

OYSTER CATCHER

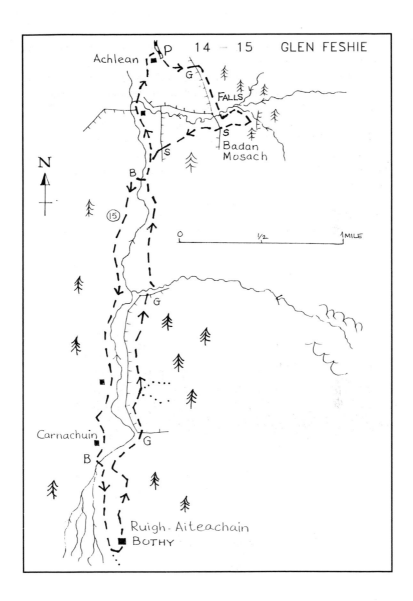

14 -- FINNEGAN'S FORCE

To be honest, there isn't a waterfall with this name -- well, not in Glen Feshie -- and its fabrication by a Southron is likely to raise the blood pressure of the average Gael to a level well above the local mountain tops, and they are very high! But the subject of this walk is so magnificent that it ought to have a name of its own, and the fact that its location is on Allt Fhearnagan should be explanation enough.

This is one of the problems with the Grampians: the magnificent is so common-place that it is often judged unworthy of any special comment, or anything other than a cursory mention on a map. There can be no other reason why this splendid waterfall has remained anonymous for so long. Where else would a tremendous double fall, cascading for hundreds of feet down a green and pleasant mountain side be virtually ignored? This is very odd, because it is one of the most easily accessible of spectacles in this most spectacular glen.

The fall is usually referred to as Badan Mosach, which is actually the name of the wooded area through which it runs, and its lack of recognition ended only recently when Louis Scott listed it in his book. It is his favourite of all the waterfalls in Scotland, and it requires very little effort to find out why.

The most convenient starting point is Achlean, where a car may be parked in the little lay-by just before the farm (NN852976). There is no doubt about the path: it is obvious, and goes off uphill to the left before the farm. This is the start of the ancient 'Foxhunters Track', which leads eventually to the summit of Carn Ban Mor. It provides a long but relatively painless route to the Sgorans, and has been a popular excursion since Victorian times; but that is a longer journey for another day. There is a ladder stile over the deer fence, and the lower track is followed, to the right, along the edge of the woodland, and straight to the bottom of the cascade.

This is the epitome of a romantic waterfall in a setting of sylvan delight. A leisurely climb to the top is a must, and will be carried out so slowly, and amidst surroundings of such sublime, enchanting and absorbing beauty, that the exertion will pass un-noticed as the falls are followed for several hundred feet uphill. The setting is a delight, and cries out for photographs as the sunlight filters through the cool mature woodland of old Scots pine, and the sights and sounds of water fill the air.

The track can be followed up until it emerges from the forest onto the open hill-side. Another track bears right, along the edge of the woodland, to the old site of an observation tower. The return track goes downhill, back to the foot of the falls, and then through a fairly new planting of Scots pines to Achleum and the river. A river-side track is then followed back to Achlean.

And the 'Force'? This is a common name for a waterfall in other parts of Britain, and is a relic of our Viking forebears. It is a corruption of the Scandanivian *fjors*, a waterfall, and it somehow seems appropriate in this place.

At the corner of the forest, by the falls, the fence has a hole that could accommodate a baby elephant (this in 1987), and some maps show a track over the moor to Achlean. Do not be tempted to take this track -- it will spoil your day. The farmer at Achlean has a special brand of invective for people who come this way, and he does have a point: fences should be crossed only via stiles or gates.

This is a really short walk, and it would have satisfied Burns, who said that Scottish waterfalls were 'worth gaun a mile tae see'. The energetic may do a few more miles by walking into the valley below Coire Gharbhlach, where there is another fall (NN875947). It is far less grand, but more remote. The route, over rather rough ground, is obvious on the 1:25000 map. A better alternative is to carry on to Landseer's Bothy.

LET US KNOW --
BEFORE YOU GO TO THE HILLS

Please complete and leave with the Police, landlady, warden, etc.
Request landlady or warden to contact Police if you are overdue

Names & Addresses: (Home & Local addresses)	Route:
Time & Date of Departure: Place of Departure:	Bad Weather Alternative:
Reg. No. of Vehicle	Where Vehicle Parked:
Estimated Time of Return:	Walking/Climbing *(delete as necessary)*

PLEASE TICK OFF EQUIPMENT CARRIED:

Waterproof Clothing *(colour:)*   Emergency Food   Ice Axe
                                               Whistle   Crampons
Winter Clothing *(colour:)*   Map Compass   Polybag
                                               Avalanche Transceiver *(Make:)*

REMEMBER --
REPORT YOUR SAFE RETURN

THIS IS VITAL IN ORDER TO AVOID NEEDLESS CONCERN FOR YOUR SAFETY.

15:-- LANDSEER'S BOTHY

In 1842 the young Queen Victoria and her Consort made their first visit to Scotland. Other visits followed, and they quite naturally came to love the place. Indeed, the spell was so strong that they had to have a permanent house there, and in 1848 they acquired the Duke of Fife's old hunting lodge at Balmoral. Thus started the tradition of regal summer holidays in the Highlands.

The Queen was very artistic, and had drawing and painting lessons from a number of artists -- Edward Lear was an early tutor, and William Leitch is the one who figured most in this role during her Balmoral days. She also had a great appreciation of the beauty of her countryside, and wished to have a permanent record of the time spent here with her beloved Albert. Over the years they compiled nine albums of drawings and water-colour paintings, which comprise a unique view of a long-vanished way of life and a seemingly immutable landscape.

A Royal commission was, apparently, a somewhat mixed blessing. It no doubt helped to further an artist's career, and it no doubt did something for his reputation, but it did not do a great deal for his pocket. The Queen is said to have not paid overmuch for the pictures she commissioned. She also knew precisely what she wanted, and the artists had to paint more or less to order. The ones who would not did not last long, and Charles Landseer, Sir Edwin's less famous brother, is a typical example. For the majority who know it, the mention of Sir Edwin Landseer's name will instantly evoke The Stag at Bay, which represents, perhaps, the pinnacle of Victorian genre painting. The original is now in Dublin, but its inspiration is all around one in Glen Feshie.

RIVER LUINEAG — LOCH MORLICH

Landseer had the ability to combine pathos with a touch of cruelty in his pictures, and he was very successful. He was one of Queen Victoria's favourites, and he visited Balmoral and other Royal estates on and off over a long period. The Queen, who was herself an accomplished water-colour painter, probably had lessons from him, too, when at Balmoral. Landseer rather enjoyed the sporting life and, although a rotten shot, he neglected no opportunity for deer stalking and similar pursuits. He certainly had a great fondness for the Highlands, where he could both indulge his tastes and soak up the atmosphere for his pictures. Glen Feshie was one of his favourite places, and he rented a bothy, or summer cottage, here from the Duchess of Bedford.

Seton Gordon, a great naturalist, author and photographer, once mentioned that a Landseer mural was still to be seen in the ruined chapel in the pinewoods beyond Glenfeshie Lodge. This was about fifty years ago. There is a mystery here. He was unlikely to make a mistake, but it is probable that what Gordon took to be a 'chapel' was, in fact, the ruin of Landseer's bothy. Now, only the chimney stack still stands, and if there was a mural on the chimney breast it is long gone. Landseer, like most Victorian landscape painters, made working drawings on the spot, using charcoal and pastels. These studies were used later, when permanent oil or water colours were worked-up in the studio. Landseer was known to try things out on the white-plastered walls, and what Gordon saw was probably the remains of some working sketches. The only certainty is that Landseer did live here for several summers, and this walk is to the site of his Highland home.

As in the previous walk, the most convenient start is from Achlean, and the route is followed past the waterfall and down to the river by Achleum. From this point, follow the river upstream for about half a mile, and cross the bridge to the other side. The river here thunders through a narrow defile, and it is worth lingering a little to enjoy the beauty and the fantasy of the natural sculptures in the water-worn rock. Carry on by the edge of the road for a mile or

Ruigh-Aiteachain
LANDSEER'S BOTHY – Glen Feshie

so to the next bridge. By the gate in the fence a notice gives details of the deer stalking: please heed it.

It should be very obvious that the road is laid on the old glacial river bed. The valley here is at least a mile wide and it must have been a magnificent stream, at least equal to the Spey. At Carnachuin, by the Stalker's house, there is a simple memorial to members of the Commando Fellcraft School which was based here in the 1940's, and there are many tales to be told of their activities in the district, both licit and otherwise. The view upstream is very grand, and is the main reason for choosing this side of the river.

Cross the bridge, and then pause by the cairn, which marks the boundary of the National Nature Reserve. It is quite usual to see groups of red deer hinds quietly grazing beyond the trees. When the wind is right it is not too difficult to get close enough for a photograph.

The track from here is obvious, and passes through some most attractive woodland to the bothy at Ruigh Aiteachain. This is one of the better bothies, and its excellent state of preservation is no doubt due, in part, to its remote position. It still looks and feels much as Bothies used to, but all too often now do not. Please remember that it is primarily a refuge and place of shelter, and bolt the door when you depart. Near by, and a little upstream, there stands an isolated chimney stack. Solidly built in local stone, it has its back to the hill, and looks over a shallow depression to the river beyond. A trickle of ice cold and delicious water runs constantly from a little spring near by, and it is easy to imagine the idyllic life here in the summer time. This is the objective of the walk, and the chimney stack is all that remains of Landseer's Bothy.

Landseer never married, but he was far from averse to feminine company, and is supposed to have had a romantic attachment to the Duchess of Bedford. It is recorded that she was a frequent visitor during the sporting season. Sir Edwin and his aristocratic landlady once were weather-bound here, and found some time to experiment in the kitchen. The result was, apparently,

'Duchesse' potatoes -- true or not, it makes a charming story.

Return to the bridge, but do not cross to Carnachuin. Keep to the right bank, and follow the riverside track to the forest fence. The path through the forest emerges by Allt Garbhlach, and the ford is some way upstream. The track continues across rough country to Achleum. There is a lot of cover on this ground, so look out for deer, and also for uncommon birds. Ospreys and eagles hunt down this glen, and there are crested tits in the pines.

From Achleum the riverside path is followed back to Achlean.

CAPERCAILLIE

FORESTS

After the last ice-age a great boreal forest spread across the northern hemisphere and literally girdled the earth. Enormous tracts of coniferous woodland still stretch across N. America and Europe, but much of the old forest has disappeared from Britain, a victim of the need for clear ground, and our apparently insatiable demand for softwood. Most of the large coniferous woodlands in Britain now are artificial, creations of the Forestry Commission and private owners, and they tend to consist of close-planted imported species of quick-growing trees. Scotland has its share of this type of woodland, and 'tax-avoidance' planting has been rapidly increasing the area that is privately owned. The plantings have often produced a characteristic blanket woodland of spindly and barren trunks rising from an apparently lifeless understory, and whilst these woodlands may be commercially valuable, they are aesthetically dead.

It is fortunate that Scotland has also retained large areas of natural pine forest, which has been the native woodland for the past few thousand years. In a few remnants of the old pine woods it is still possible to get an idea of how the country must have looked before the onset of man.

The largest surviving areas are to be found in and about the Cairngorms country, typically in the forests of Abernethy, Rothiemurchus, Glen More, Glen Feshie and Glen Lui. Most of these old woods of Caledon have been worked commercially, and they no longer truly represent the wild country of long ago, but they do have an oddly primeval feel, and provide a real flavour of the past.

Juniper, Scots pine and yew are the only three conifers now indigenous to Britain. Spruce was once a native tree, but it became extinct, and all the existing trees have been generated from imported stock. The old forest remnants consist mainly of native Scots pine and juniper, with thickets of silver birch and rowans, and some alder and willow scrub. The tree spacing varies, but it is nowhere very dense, and old trees usually lie and rot where they have fallen.

In many areas the regeneration of the trees seems good, despite the deer, and there is also a large, rich and varied assortment of plants, animals and insects in a deep and colourful understory that flourishes only where there is sufficient light.

The WITCH'S TREE – Queen's Forest

The Scots pine is a most interesting tree and is tremendously varied in appearance depending on its age. Young and immature trees are quite undistinguished, with greyish bark, dark green needles and a roughly conical shape. As such there is little to distinguish them from many other conifers. With maturity comes a contrast so great that the old trees might be easily mistaken for a different species. There is probably no more more beautiful and majestic tree than a mature Scots pine, with its new bark shining like freshly etched and beaten copper in the bright sunshine of a spring day. Those noble old trees display venerable age in every crack, crease, wrinkle and furrow of their lower trunks. Higher up, the new bark glows beneath large umbrellas of the darkest green, and the needled canopies provide a perfect foil for the yellow pollened spikes of the new cones.

Although 'forest' tends to evoke an area of woodland, there is another much older meaning of the word, and it crops up a lot in Scotland. Traditionally all land set aside for hunting deer and game is designated 'forest', and this includes the rough hill and moor country frequented by red deer. The forests of Upper Glen Avon, of Mar and of Gaick are all typical and local examples of this. This distinction is recognised in this book, and is the reason why the Lairig Ghru is included with the Forest Walks.

NOTE: The local forests are working woodlands where timber is a crop. Work is always in progress somewhere, and this can mean that a path or forest road shown on the map may be temporarily closed. This is for your safety. The Visitor Centres know the current situation and will always offer advice if asked.

16:- WAYFARING

There is a Wayfaring course in the Queen's Forest, and a cheap Wayfaring Package can be bought from many outlets in the area. The main components are an excellent map of the forest -- large scale and very detailed -- some general notes, and information about Wayfaring and suggestions about how to get started. Equipped with this map and a compass it is possible to wander about in the forest without using any of the forest-walk paths. If you really want to learn to read a map and use a compass, this is the ideal way to do it.

To give some sense of purpose, go along the ski road to the picnic area car park, on the right, just beyond the Allt Mor bridge (NH980092). A master map is displayed there with the Wayfaring controls marked on it. The controls are wooden posts with a distinctive symbol and code letters painted on the top, and the idea is to mark-up your own map with the locations and numbers, and then seek them out on the ground. Complete instructions come with the map. It is really Orienteering, but a lot more relaxed. If you go round the controls and keep a note, you can send off and get a diploma from the Inverness Orienteering Club. It looks impressive!

It is a different world in the forest, and it isn't just a lot of trees. There are rare flowers and birds, dramatic ravines and secret lochans. There are no routes -- you make your own -- and there is a lot of quiet satisfaction and a real sense of achievement to be had in navigating from point to point in what is, after all, a quite bewildering terrain. Be prepared for funny looks from the ordinary walkers you will see from time to time as you burst out of the forest, cross one of the tracks, and disappear into the undergrowth on the other side. And if you dress discreetly and move quietly you could see a lot of unusual wildlife.

PEREGRINE

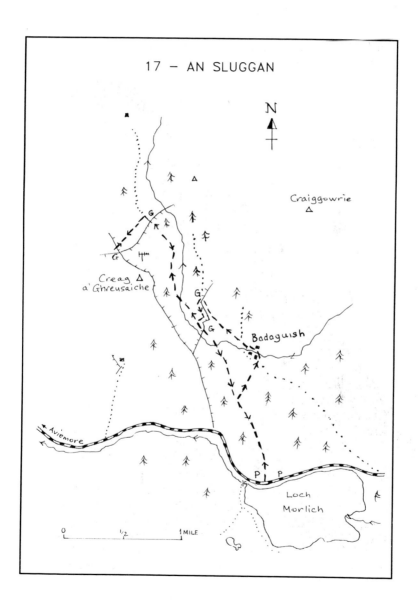

17 – AN SLUGGAN

N

Craiggowrie
△

Creag △
a' Ghreusaiche

G

G

G
G

Badaguish

Aviemore

P P

Loch
Morlich

0   ½   1 MILE

17-- AN SLUGGAN

The origin of this rough old track is not clear, but it is certainly an ancient right-of-way from Glen More towards the Speyside road to Boat of Garten and beyond, which it joins near the old church of Kincardine (NH939155). If it was originally a way to the church it must be very old, because the original building was destroyed in the 15th century when the Grants burned it, complete with a complement of sheltering Comyns, in the sort of tit-for-tat reprisal that seems to have been a quite common occurence in the Scotland of those days. The church was re-built only about 100 years ago.

Far more likely, then, is that An Sluggan was a convenient route to the ferry, cutting off, as it does, a long detour via Coylumbridge and Loch Pityoulish. Modern walkers can use it for the same purpose. Sluggan apparently means 'gullet', and the pass is aptly named from the narrow defile traversed high above the burn betwen Creag Mheadhonach and Creag a' Ghreusaiche (TV Hill). This 6 mile walk does not go all the way to the church, although that is an option open to the individual, rather, it is a gentle stroll to the 'TV Hill' with opportunities for plenty of bird-watching.

Some authorities would have us believe that the bird-watching 'Mecca' is Loch Garten. This is not so, not even for those whose main interest is the osprey, but the R.S.P.B. maintain the fiction because it is useful: it keeps up the number of paying visitors at the Reserve, and it diverts attention from the many other ospreys that nest elsewhere. The osprey population in NE Scotland is now quite large, and most of them don't nest at Loch Garten. Some ospreys do nest very near to Aviemore, and they often fish the local waters. In addition, these local woodlands provide an ideal habitat for many other birds that are uncommon elsewhere: crested tits, capercailles and crossbills, for example.

Park at the picnic area at the W end of Loch Morlich (NH958096), and head N along the sign-posted track, immediately across the road. The way is through a woodland of mixed conifers: some native Scots pine and some imported species. After about 3/4 of a mile, a track to the right goes off to Badaguish, which has been given a new lease of life, and is a holiday centre for handicapped children. A detour via Bagaduish will add about a mile, but is worthwhile for the wealth of small birds in the vicinity. At Bagaduish follow the track round past the pond and the bungalows, cross the little bridge over the stream, and then keep left. Do not go along the road to the right. As the road climbs away from the settlement there is a gate in the fence, and immediately beyond this a faint but definite track doubles away downhill to the Sluggan road, which is followed to the right.

At the top of the pass, by the cairn, a track goes off left up to the TV mast and the repeater station. Stay away from these, and carry on through the gate in the forest fence. Just to the right a venerable old pine makes a 'V' on top of a little knoll, and there is a magnificent view of the country to the north. Go left, uphill, on the barely visible remnants of an old track. At the crest of the ridge, by the fence, there is an old wall with an ancient, dated boundary stone. To the left is the summit of Creag a' Ghreusaiche (The Cobbler's Crag). A magnificent panorama is revealed, with the whole of Speyside visible to the N, and the grand expanse of the Monadliaths, Glen Einich, Rothiemurchus and the Cairngorms, sweeping round from behind Aviemore, not so far away in the west.

There is a grandstand view of the moor below, and this is a good place in which to settle and watch, through binoculars, the wildlife at the forest margins.This is also a good place for watching moorland birds, which range from curlews and plovers to merlins, or were they harriers? Ospreys sometimes wheel above the hill, which seems to be immediately below a flight path to the rich fishing ground of Loch Morlich. There is always something of interest, and always something new.

Go back to the Sluggan track, and straight down the road to the car park. Some time spent observing the loch here will often bring a reward in the form of fishing ospreys.

RED DEER

18 – THE LAIRIG GHRU

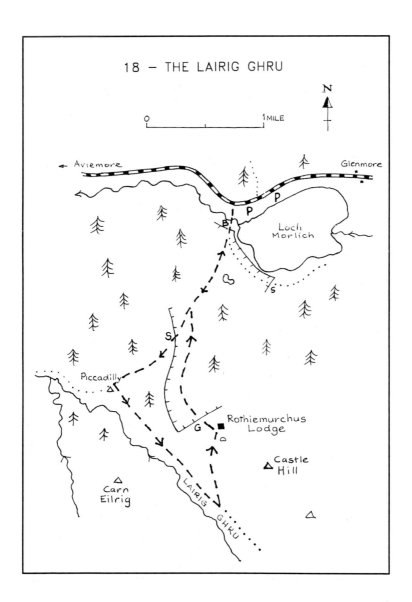

18:--TO THE LAIRIG GHRU

The shape of the landscape in these highlands is mostly the result of glacial action. The mountains were sculpted and the valleys excavated by the relentless grinding of the ice. Frost, snow, wind and water continue the process, and the result is a wild and romantic countryside.

A great ice-gouged valley runs from Blair Atholl to its junction with the Dee at White Bridge near Braemar. The northwards continuation of the valley towards Aviemore is the Lairig Ghru, which transects the Cairngorms' highest peaks.

This walk, which is a round trip from Loch Morlich, goes to the pass and traverses some rugged but beautiful country. The scenery is varied and dramatic, the distance is about five miles, and the walk will take about three hours.

Take the A951 ski road out of Aviemore to the first picnic area and car park at the beginning of the loch (NH958097). Cross the Bailey Bridge over the Luineag, and walk up the road towards Rothiemurchus Lodge. Follow the track to the right at the junction sign-posted for Piccadilly, and cross the deer fence at the stile with the dog flap in it. As the fence starts to bear off to the left it takes the new planting with it, and the path goes ever more deeply into the old forest.

The path starts to go quite steeply downhill, and just after this a sylvan glade opens up to the left: tread lightly and quietly now, for this glade is a favourite haunt of deer. When the wind is southerly and there is no-one else about, it can be most rewarding in this spot. If a browsing roebuck senses an intruder and barks, you bark back from cover, and wait. Roe deer are quite inquisitive, and he might come over for a closer look.

The track continues to a cross-roads in the forest where there is a large National Nature Reserve cairn, and, maybe, a signboard pointing to Braemar. Piccadilly was, at one time, a most important junction. The Lairig track continued N to cross the Luineag by a pine-log bridge to Coylum Bridge and beyond, and a branch of the track, by the river, went E to Medicine Well, Ruaran Raoin Fhraoich (O.S. Rinraoaich), which drew visitors from as far afield as Braemar.

The E-W road which crosses here is the old Thieves Road, used by the caterans of Lochaber on their forays into the fat cattle lands of Banff and Moray.

Apart from the road surface, the country here is probably little altered since those times, and it should be savoured, for this is the oldest, and the largest, and the least changed remnant of the ancient woodlands of Britain. It is something to be cherished, and it is a privilege to walk here.

Take the track S towards Braemar. The surrounding woodland becomes progressively more beautiful as the path ascends, and Carn Eilrig is prominent to the right, across the valley of the Allt Druidh. As the woodland starts to peter out, the scenery all about is an assault on the senses, so theatrical are the views.

Behind, below, and to the right, the river courses through a gorge clothed densely in variegated woodland. Ahead, the sheer-walled pass between the mountains beckons, or threatens, according to the weather. This is the fringe of the forest, and as the path climbs higher on to the open moor, the woodland clings to the shelter of the deeply-cut valley sides. Across the valley, the E flanks of Carn Eilrig are often speckled with grazing deer.

The general beauty of the place was recognised by those great artists, the Ordnance Survey cartographers, and the old map of Aviemore and the Cairngorms had a striking drawing of a cock capercaillie against the background of a delightful and intriguing river valley. The viewpoint for this scene is about NH904067, just to the side of, and below the path.

Where a track cuts in from the left, bear left away from the Lairig and follow the path across the flank of Castle Hill up to Rothiemurchus Lodge. The way from here curves round to the left, and then goes strongly downhill, past Lochan nan Geadas, and back to the car park.

REDSHANK

19 — A FOREST WALK

19:-- A WALK IN THE FOREST

Almost opposite the road end at Coylumbridge (NH915107) is the effective start, or finish, of the Lairig Ghru. It looks just like an unmade road, with a caravan site down by the river to the left, but this is an illusion, and it is much more than that: it is the entrance to an enchanted world.

Rothiemurchus is really quite incredible -- it is just one of several old boreal forest remnants in this part of the world, and it is certainly the most accessible, yet it has as much impact, and more raw, primeval feel, than all the others put together. If you want to know what virgin pine forest is really like, then this 5 mile walk is for you.

Immediately through the gate there is a different world, and the transition from open country is abrupt. This is a mixed woodland, and roe deer could be grazing quite unseen on the right, only a few yards from the track. Lairig Ghru Cottage, on the left, is a cheerful and most photogenic log cabin, which marks the end of civilisation until Braemar.

The landscape here is varied, and the dense and distinctly wild woodland to the right is in marked contrast to the cool green grassland down by the river. The rough track of cobbles and pink granite sand divides the two, and don't be afraid to deviate from the road and explore a little way along the animal tracks that lead off on either side. This is moth country, too, and entomologists come from far and wide to study these rare, but often rather drab, denizens of the pine woods.

In a little while the forest thins, and near a big cairn there is a parting of the ways. The track branches to the right, and it is marked for Glen Einich and Loch an Eilein. The woodland gives way to a rough scrubland of grass, heather, and various mosses, dotted here and there with junipers and a few trees, and the land rises a little towards the old farmstead of Whitewell.

There is dense forest away to the right, and the dark and dramatic cone of Carn Eilrig is prominent to the S, where it guards the entrances to Glen Einich and the Lairig Ghru.

The maze of tracks to left and right can be ignored, but back in the woodland, beyond the fence, and about 2 miles from the start, a major forest road cuts across to right and left (NH916079). This is a stretch of the ancient Rathad Nam Mearlach -- the Thieves Road -- used by the Lochaber freebooters on their cattle rustling forays into the rich country to the east. Their route is now followed to the left, but pause a while at little Lochan Deo, tucked away and partly hidden, just by the junction of the roads.

The way goes now through increasingly splendid country to the river, which is reached at the Cairngorm Club Bridge. The original ford is close by the bridge, on the right, and it must have been a rough old crossing when the melt was flowing well. The water is delicious and is always icy cold. It is worthwhile going upstream a short distance to the confluence of the Druidh and Am Beanaidh. This is majestic country, but often harsh and wild: witness the testament of the fallen trees. These have been literally torn out by the roots, victims of some incredibly violent winter gales. Wind speeds of 172 m.p.h. were recorded on Cairngorm in 1987 -- twice as violent as those that devastated the English woodlands!

Go back now to the junction about a quarter of a mile away, and take the right branch of the Lairig Ghru track that follows the forest margin close by the river. The outward route is rejoined at the cairn, and the road is not then far away. Coylumbridge Hotel is just a couple of hundred yards down the road to Aviemore, and a dram, or a long cool pint, or both, in Walkers will provide a fitting conclusion to the walk. Have a look at the roadside below the pines in the hotel grounds. It is absolutely littered with the gnawed remains of pine cones. This is the work of the many hungry red squirrels with which the area abounds. The 'pineapple' top is the giveaway -- field mice eat the lot.

20 — CRAIGELLACHIE

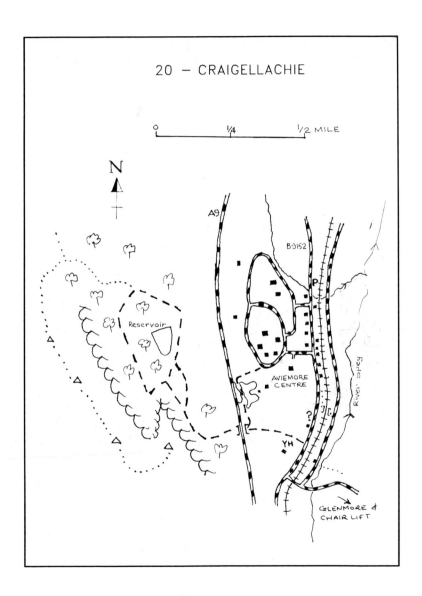

20 -- CRAIGELLACHIE

Craigellachie is the well-wooded low hill with the sheer and craggy rock-face that provides such an impressive natural setting for the Aviemore Centre. It is this rock, and not the fishing town in lower Strathspey, that figures in the Grant motto *Stand Fast, Craigellachie!* That Craigellachie endures is beyond doubt, and it is central to the little National Nature Reserve, which covers about 2 square miles of delectable low hill country to the W of Aviemore. The reserve is notable on many counts, one of which is a resident pair of peregrine falcons. The Reserve has a large area of birch scrub, which is a habitat for many species of birds uncommon elsewhere in the area, for some reptiles and small mammals which are common but rarely seen, and for a variety of insect life that would be unusual anywhere, and which attracts naturalists from everywhere. It is strange that an area so delightful in itself is not over-run with other visitors, and not least of the delights of time spent here is that one rarely sees many other people. It is a little haven on the edge of the town, and most of the visitors encountered here seem to be specialist ornithologists, or other naturalists. This isolation is probably due to a combination of things, like the A9 which separates it from the town, general ignorance of the access tunnel's whereabouts, and lack of publicity.

Two paths lead to the tunnel, which was provided as the only access point when the A9 by-passed the town some years ago. One path runs from the main street, from a point between the Youth Hostel and a caravan site at NH894118. The other path, which is signposted, starts from a bend in a road on the Aviemore Centre, near to the Badenoch Hotel at NH893123. It goes across the grass by the fishing school loch, and picks up the other path near to the tunnel.

Various short walks are possible in the reserve, and some are shown on the map. You will soon create your own favourites, but the wisest course on a first visit is probably to follow a clockwise course on the finely graded path around the nature trail. This is constructed of gravel, stone slabs and duck-boarding, depending on the terrain. It is beautifully done and maintained, and the 'viewpoints' are well chosen. There is nothing here of the artificiality so often evident on other nature trails. No numbered posts and set pieces, and, apart from the path, it is all as nature made it. An explanatory leaflet can be had from the Tourist Information Office, and it is cheap and excellent, but the lack of the leaflet is no obstacle to enjoyment and understanding.

At the end of the upper leg, where the trail turns downhill towards the reservoir, a path goes on and uphill left on to the ridge. This is an excellent extension, which offers even better views of the Cairngorms, but PLEASE DO NOT GO UP HERE IN APRIL AND JULY -- you could disturb the peregrines at what are sensitive times in their breeding cycle.

The birch is a widespread and hardy tree, and several species grow naturally in Britain. Silver birch is an import that has spread widely and hybridised with other trees, and it is a graceful and beautiful species that enhances any area in which it grows. The woodland here is a rare and precious gem, and one which makes a very refreshing change from the seemingly ubiquitous conifers elsewhere. Autumn is a particularly splendid season, and the reserve is especially beautiful then, as the turning leaves, when sunlit, provide a green, grey and gilded tapestry which is a vivid and unforgettable backdrop to the town. The quiet and contemplative stroller here will be rewarded with the sight and sounds of many unusual birds, moths, small animals and plants. It is all the more attractive for the marked contrast with the great pine forests nearby. Wander and wonder, and haste ye back!

MONUMENTS

The Cairngorms are unique. A combination of geology and climate has ensured that no other mountains have their particular attributes. This is well known, but there is another aspect of this particular bit of the Grampians, that is, at least, unusual. There is no modern counterpart in any of the other mountain regions of Britain, yet it seems not to have been remarked upon as a whole. The oddity is the sheer quantity and variety of memorials which, in some places, seem literally to litter the landscape. This is a comment, not a complaint, and it must be said that, in general, the monoliths, obelisks, steles and other stones, that some people have erected, usually as memorials to other people, and who were only rarely locals, are never incongruous, and they usually blend quite naturally into the hillsides or woodlands which they adorn.

Some of the memorials are natural and not man-made. These are the stones -- sometimes glacial erratics -- which are so large or so prominent that they have been given a particular name, as is the Gaelic way. *Clach Mhic Cailein* -- the Argyll Stone of the Sgorrans -- is a typical example. In other cases a natural stone has been transported and embroidered for a particular purpose such is the Norwegian Stone of Glen More. There are others. The following list gives the names and O.S. map references of a baker's dozen of the Cairngorm's many monuments and memorials:

The memorial at Rynettin (NJ012138) is a white granite stone, on a knoll just to the W of the road. It is dedicated to one James Hamilton Maxwell, a young man from Edinburgh, who was killed at Ypres during the Great War of 1914-1918.

Close to the Cairngorm Club bridge, in Rothiemurchus

(NH926079), a pink granite stone commemorates a casualty of a 'V1' flying bomb attack on London, in 1943.

At the Loch an Eilein branch on the Feshiebridge Road (NH891097) there is an elaborate monument to Dr. Martineau, who once spent his summers at Polchar, close by. He was a Victorian clergyman, and like many churchmen of his time, did not confine his activities to the church. He founded a local library and a craft school, and he also secured general access to much of the local forest: no mean achievement in those days. His sister Harriet was an equally formidable Victorian lady. In her day she was a famous writer of improving tales, but she is now chiefly remembered for an excellent guide to the English Lake District.

The Norwegian Stone, in Glenmore (NH976098), is a memorial to the members of Kompani Linge, the Norwegian Commandos who carried out the Telemark Raid during the last Great War -- see Walk Number One.

In the Queen's Forest, near to one of the controls on the Wayfaring Course, there is a cluster of tombstones on a knoll (NH987092). It is a turn-of-the-century graveyard for the dogs of the Deniston family then resident at Glenmore Lodge -- the present Youth Hostel.

At the foot of Tor Alvie (NH869077), amongst the birches of Kinrara, and just across the river from Inchriach, a simple granite obelisk is dedicated to the memory of Jane, Duchess of Gordon in the reign of George III.

At the top of Tor Alvie (NH878089), the last Duke of Gordon has a splendid pillar as his personal monument.

Close by, still on top of Tor Alvie (NH873086), there is a Waterloo cairn. It is a reminder of the battle, not the station!

Back across the Spey, near the W end of Loch an Eilean (NH898078), yet another granite slab is a memorial for General Rice. This poor soul met **his** Waterloo when he fell through the ice and drowned whilst ice skating on Boxing Day, in 1892.

Kennapole Hill, which rises from the W end of Loch an

Eilean, is crowned by a cairn which commemorates a Duchess of Bedford (NH886071).

On Creag Dhubh, on the run up to the Sgorrans, S of Loch an Eilean, and to the W of the Glen Einich track (NH905040), Clach Mhic Cailein -- The Argyll Stone -- is a granite lump from which the eponymous Earl is said to have seen the mountains of Argyll when fleeing from his defeat in Glen Livet in 1594. It is probable that he came this way, and as Cruachan Ben can be seen from Carn Ban Mor, there may be more than legend to the name.

About half a mile to the S, on the same stony ridge (NH903034), another tor is sometimes called the Atholl Stone.

Down the Feshie, just by the bridge at Carnachuin (NH846939) there is a memorial to the members of the Highland Fieldcraft Training Centre, founded by Lord Rowallen as a training cadre for potential officers during the war of 1939-1945. It was the forerunner of the modern 'Outbound Schools'.

When all else palls, or simply if the fancy takes one, a short walk can be based on a visit to any one of these artefacts. The 1:25000 map is ideal for route planning, and don't forget to take a camera.

SAFETY IN THE HILLS

Throughout the winter these mountains are not for the ordinary walker. In May there can still be deep snow cover and occasional blizzards on the high plateaux, but the weather then is not as severe as winter in the English hills, although many of the N facing gullies and sheltered spots retain some snow throughout the summer. I once walked a party along Cairngorm's N ridge when it was overlaid with a foot of snow. There was thick mist and it was cold, and at mid-day it started to snow. We walked on compass bearings, and were at Eagle's Corrie before we came out of the clouds and that was on the 1st of June! In that sort of weather it is better to stay in the woods, or on the lower hills.

Major causes of accidents are avalanches, uncontrolled slides on snow slopes or ice-covered grass, and falls through cornices and snow bridges over streams. There is also the danger of stumbling on boulders in deep snow or heather. These are major hazards in early spring, but they can all be avoided by sensible choice of routes. Remember that rock-climbing is a specialist sport. Causes of difficulty include under-estimation of the time needed for a walk, slow companions, and unwise eating and drinking -- a little and often is a good rule.

Exposure is another danger, and it is all too easy to under-estimate the extent of the climatic change between the valleys and the high tops. Allow also for the chilling effect of wind when one is wet. Adequate clothing must be worn, and extra warm clothing carried. Do not omit a pair of sunglasses, and wear them on snowfields, especially if the sky is overcast.

It is important to obey the following rules:

Do not walk alone on the high tops.

Be adequately clothed, and shod, and carry spare warm clothing, a survival bag and a pair of sun-glasses.

Carry a whistle, a torch, a compass and a map, and know how to use them.

Carry an emergency food supply: something light and energy-providing, e.g. raisins, chocolate or mint cake.

Constantly take note of where you are. This will be useful if a mist comes down, or if it starts to snow heavily.

Abandon your walk if bad weather clamps down.

Leave a note of your route and bad weather alternative, and your expected time of return.

Do not deviate from your plan.

Northern Constabulary are the co-ordinators for Mountain Rescue in the area, and they have produced a special route form which is available at most of the places where people stay. Please use it. It is important to announce your safe return. This will avoid needless anxiety and a possible false alarm. Remember that the idea is to cater for the abnormal. It isn't clever to ignore these precautions: it is stupid and could cost lives.

For Mountain Rescue and other emergencies: Tel. Aviemore 810222

NATURAL HISTORY NOTES

The countryside around Aviemore provides a wide variety of habitats, each of which has its own distinctive population, and these notes do not pretend to be anything other than a cursory comment on the unusual. The natural history of the region is the subject of a classic work, *The Cairngorms* which should be read by all those with more than just a passing interest in the area. The Forestry Commission guide to Glenmore Forest Park, which contains a wealth of related information, is also still in print, and both books are remarkably cheap.

Many other books offer information about the locality and its inhabitants, and a few offer advice on how to observe them. As with many other things, an ounce of practice is worth a ton of theory, and the best thing is to go for a quiet walk and start looking.

It would be most unusual to spend any time in the hills, away from the Cairngorm Plateau, and not come across some red deer. Fences exclude them from much of the woodland, but they are occasionally seen in Rothiemurchus, near Piccadilly, in the plantation near Badaguish, and in the woodland between Glenmore and the ski lift. In the early morning -- about 6 a.m. -- groups are often to be seen grazing around the caravans and tents on the camp site in Glenmore. Opposite sexes live separate lives through most of the year and come together only in the breeding season, about October.

Roe deer live in small family groups, and are wholly creatures of the woodland. They are very common in this area, and they do a good deal of damage to seedling trees.

Reindeer are different in every way. Orginally resident here in ancient times, they became extinct along with the wild boars and the wolves. Mr. Mikel Utse, a Swedish Lapp, visited Aviemore in 1947 and decided that it was reindeer country. He won a long battle against the bureaucrats and introduced the first beasts about 1952. After a series of reverses the animals have settled down, and their numbers increased, but now there are problems once again, and 10% of the herd is lost each year! Many of the people who go on to the hills take drinks with them in metal cans. When some people have had their drink, they flatten the can and throw it away. A reindeer may lick this, and the can then lodges at the back of the reindeer's throat. The animal doesn't choke: it simply starves to death. If you have a drink on the hill and are tempted to throw the can away, please think again. You could cost an animal its life.

Each day, at about 11 a.m., Mr. Smith, the owner, takes a party of visitors to a herd pastured near Glenmore, but many animals roam freely in the hills. They have been seen at the S end of the Lairig Ghru, the far side of Lairig an Laoigh, in Strath Nethy and on the plateaux of Cairngorm and Braeriach. They may be encountered almost anywhere on the hill, and brief acquaintance will show why they are beloved by the Lapps. Normally they are delightfully friendly and gentle beasts, and they seem to like the company of people. But do be careful: the bulls can be quite ferocious during the autumn rut, and paired animals, like Garbo, just want to be left alone.

A wild cat is not a domestic tabby gone wrong: it is a distinctive and very handsome breed of cat that is well established in Glenmore and Rothiemurchus. They are nocturnal and very shy, and unlikely to be seen other than by accident, or during a visit to the Wildlife Park at Kincraig.

Blue, or mountain, hares are smaller than their lowland cousins, and they assume a white coat for the winter. They seem to be quite rare now, but have been seen above the Ryvoan Pass, near Lochan na Beinne, and over on the Bynacks.

The variety and number of birds is enormous, but luck must

play a part in the sighting of the rarities. The capercaille is a large and ungainly bird which does not seem to fly well. It is more likely to be heard than seen, and in flight it looks like a black or brown turkey (the hens are brown). Rothiemurchus, near Piccadilly, and An Sluggan, near Badaguish, are known habitats. Blackcock were common many years ago, but now seem to be rare. They like to inhabit the country at forest margins, where old woodland gives way to pasture. Modern forestry, and the spread of new plantations have reduced the area of this type of habitat, and this may be a reason for their decline. Abernethy and the W end of the Queen's Forest, around An Sluggan, seem to be localities where they might still be found.

Crossbills, tree creepers, long tailed and crested tits, siskins and woodpeckers may all be observed in the woods, and it is impossible to ignore the chaffinches, which flock around the clearings and in the car parks. A little patience and some crumbs should ensure some delightful photographs. Some ornithologists maintain that the local birds have their own particular dialect.

Away from the woods, red grouse live on the lower hills, and ptarmigan occur above 3000 feet. Their nests are just scrapes in the ground, usually on the lee side of a rock. Golden eagles may be seen sometimes about Strath Nethy, the Lairig Ghru and down the Feshie, but people disturb them, and they may be deserting the area now that it is becoming so popular. Dotterel may be seen on Cairngorm plateau above the head of Loch Avon.

At Craigellachie, behind the Aviemore Centre, there is one of the most consistently successful peregrine breeding sites in Britain, and it is comparatively easy to enjoy the thrilling and rewarding sight of one of these marvellous falcons in flight, perhaps returning with a kill. Many people travel long distances to see these birds, and it was a surprise to learn recently that Britain now has one of the major populations. It was said, for instance, that only seventy are left in the whole of France.

For many visitors the great attraction now is the ospreys,

which sometimes seem to be everywhere. It may be a premature speculation, but their population seems to be increasing quite quickly, and sightings are commonplace in certain areas. At least one pair of birds is resident near Loch Morlich, and often can be seen fishing the Loch. They are from a local nest which has been used on and off for some twenty years. Five ospreys -- two pairs and a loner -- have been observed apparently fighting for possession of this nest. All very exciting. Another osprey, with a liking for Loch a' Gharbh Choire, probably spends the summer in the Braes of Abernethy. This area has now been bought by the R.S.P.B, so its future may be secure.

The plant life of the region is as varied as the terrain, and uncommon varieties at low level include lousewort, chickweed-wintergreen, twinflower, butterwort and sundews. Cow-, crow-and cloud-berries, creeping azalea, alpine lady's mantle, saxifrages, moss campion, and a positively bewildering array of mosses and lichens may all be found at higher altitudes.

The local woodlands are a veritable paradise for entomologists, and contain a wealth of moths, mosquitoes, midges, gnats, flies, mites, beetles, bugs, spiders, centipedes, millipedes, ants, and a whole host of weird and wonderful insects, many of them rare, and many of them to be found nowhere else. A famous naturalist was once asked if his life's work had taught him anything about God. 'Yes', he is said to have replied, 'He is inordinately fond of beetles!' In the country about Aviemore one can see the point. Superficially the forest floor is virtually dead, and nothing stirs on the surface other than the odd wood ant, and ground, dung, tiger and rove beetles. Lift the litter a little, and it is a totally different world: a savage and violent jungle, where eat or be eaten is the rule. Wood ant nests cannot be ignored, and these remarkable mounds of millions of pine needles house vast numbers of these busy creatures. Please do not disturb them: it could do irreparable harm.

Most people seem to actively dislike insects, and dismiss them all as 'creepy crawlies', which is sad, for they are all interesting animals. One may, perhaps make an exception in the case of midges, which are normally only of interest to anglers, fish, birds and bats. To everybody else they are irritating, in both meanings of the word, and are an unmitigated and uncontrollable nuisance.

FURTHER READING

The heyday of Cairngorm and Speyside literature seems to have been the Victorian era, but most of what was written then is now out of print. Seton Gordon wrote excellent books over a period of some 50 years from the 1920's on. Many of them are about the Cairngorms and their wildlife, and they can sometimes be found in the second-hand market. They are all good reading. The following more recent works may also be of interest to readers who wish to learn more about the region:

The Cairngorms. D. Nethersole-Thompson and A. Watson. New and enlarged edition, Melven Press, Perth, 1982. ISBN 1 906664 12 8. An exhaustive and very readable study of the physical and natural features of the region. This is a superb book, and it is very cheap.

Glenmore Forest Park Cairngorms. Forestry Commission. HMSO 1975. This guide to the many attractions of this particular glen is a 'must' for anyone holidaying in the area, and is fantastic value at £1:00.

Successful Nature Watching. Hall/Cleave/Sturry. Hamlyn, 1985. ISBN 0 600 30602 X. One of a number of books on the subject, this is a useful guide to habitats and techniques, and is reasonably priced.

Collins New Naturalist series is being re-printed in paperback, and they are incomparable books for the serious naturalist. *Mountains and Moorlands*, by W.H. Pearsall, is especially recommended.

The Highlands and Islands Development Board have also published a series of large-format paperbacks on specialist topics, such as Birds, The Highlands, Mountain Flowers, etc. They cover the whole of the Highlands, and are well worth having.

USEFUL INFORMATION

ACCOMMODATION: This does not normally present a problem, and there is adequate accommodation of all types and at all prices, including camping on the site in Glenmore, self-catering in the Aviemore Chalets Motel, B. & B. in private houses, Youth Hostels at Aviemore and Loch Morlich, and the comforts of the plush hotels in the Aviemore Centre and at Coylumbridge, and timeshare developments which seem to be growing like mushrooms all over the place. A new and very attractive venture is the privately-owned Glen Feshie Hostel, near Kincraig, for cheaper, and family, accommodation.

Kingussie has a wealth of accommodation of all types, and this pleasant Highland town has much to recommend it as a holiday centre. It is a convenient base for the Cairngorms, and its proximity to Loch Insh, Glen Feshie and the beautiful, lonely, and rather neglected Monadliaths, are added attractions. It is remote from the frantic bustle of the Aviemore Centre, and some may regard this as a bonus.

Boat of Garten, Carrbridge, Nethy Bridge and Grantown are all within reasonable distance for the motorist, and all have something to offer other than a bed. There is normally no need for advance booking outside the skiing season, and at Bank Holiday week-ends.

The best plan for casuals is to go to the nearest Tourist Information Centre and take advantage of the excellent booking service. Ring Aviemore 810363.

The Scottish Tourist Board does an excellent glossy brochure every year.

TRANSPORT: Most visitors arrive by car, and car parks are plentiful. There is an infrequent bus service from Aviemore to the ski lift. The bus runs from the railway station in Aviemore and operates throughout the year, other than in the autumn between October and

December. Taxis are plentiful, and are a cheaper alternative for four people. **Bill's Taxis** is particularly good --Aviemore 811105.

Mountain bikes have become cult machines, but they do provide an excellent means of getting to the most unlikely places. They can be hired at **Highland Guides** and at the **Visitors' Centre** at Inverdruie, from **Cairdsport**, and from **Bill Wilson's Shop** in Glenmore. Models vary, and have from 18 to 21 gears! Prices also vary, and range from £5 - £10 per day. If this sounds a lot, remember that they are **very** expensive, and get a lot of very hard use.

REFRESHMENTS: It would be unreasonable to expect much in the mountains (this is not the Alps, after all!) but there are basic cafes at each of the stations on the chairlift. There is a cafe at the shop in Glenmore, and this pleasant oasis at the head of the glen is highly recommended. Also recommended is '**Walkers'** at Coylumbridge Hotel. A drink and a reasonable meal can be enjoyed there at virtually any time in very civilised surroundings. Three cheers for sensible licensing laws!

ACCESS: The Highland Scots have a very liberal attitude to strangers walking across their land, although some of the incomers from outwith Scotland can have an odd attitude. There is no law of trespass as such in Scotland, and there should be no problem on any of the low-level walks, providing that you are not carrying a fishing rod or gun. That could be construed as 'trespass in pursuit of game', and that is a serious offence. There are restricted areas on the hills during the deer cull, roughly from mid-August to the end of October. Any of the Information Centres will have details, or ring Aviemore 810287, 810250 or 810477. This is essential, chiefly for your own safety!

WEATHER FORECASTS: Can be obtained from the Visitor Centre at Inverdruie and the sign board at the Chairlift Station. The Met. Office have a National Service, and the Grampian number is 0898-500-424. It costs about £1! There is probably a local service on 8091 or 8092.

GAELIC GLOSSARY

Gaelic names tend to relate to the appearances or associations of things, a laudable and useful practice, which means that an elementary knowledge of some words can add to the information we derive from the map. For example, *Coire an Lochain* is a rocky hollow with a small lake -- an exact and economical description.

This is not the only benefit, but it does mean that we do not have to bother so much about pronunciation, the rules for which are complicated, to say the least. The worst problem concerns the aspirated diagraphs, *mh* and *bh*, which are pronounced as 'V' at the beginning of a word, and are virtually silent in the middle and at the end of a word, as also are *dh* and *th*.

Aber, Abar, Obar: River estuary
Abhainn: River (arn)
Allt, Ald, Ault: Burn (Stream)
Aonach: Ridge
Argiod: Silver
Aviemore: Great Slope
Badaguish: Clump of pine trees (badwish)
Badan Mosach: Nasty little clump of trees
Ban: White
Beag: Little
Bealach: Pass
Beinn, Ben: Mountain
Beith: Birch tree
Bhuachaille, Buchaille: Shepherd, herdsman (vuckle, buckle)
Bidean: Pinnacle
Bodach: Old man

Brae: Slope
Buidhe: Yellow (Bweeth)
Caber: Tree
Cas: Steep
Chalamain: Pigeons
Chait: Cat
Ciste: Box (kissed)
Clach: Stone
Cnap: Knob, Hillock (crap)
Coire, Choire: Rocky Hollow (corry)
Creag: Cliff
Darroch: Oak
Dearg: Red (jarrag)
Doire: Grove, hollow
Druidh: Shieling (drewy)
Druim: Ridge
Dubh: Black
Eag: Notch
Eagach: Notched
Eas: Waterfall
Eilean: Island
Eilrig: Deer walk
Fiacaill: Teeth (fyckle)
Frithe: Forest (free)
Gall: Strangers
Gabhar, Ghobhar: Goat (gower)
Garbh: Rough
Geadas: Pike
Ghru: Grim, forbidding
Gleann: Narrow valley, glen
Gorm: Blue, azure, green
Gowrie: Goats
Inver: River bank
Iolaire: Eagles

Lairig: Pass
Laoigh: Calves (loig)
Leth-Choin: Lurcher dog
Liath: Grey
Linne: Pool
Lochan: Small lake
Loisgte: Burnt
Luineag: Surging
Mam: Round hill
Meall: Knob, hump
Mhadaidh: Fox (vatee)
Mheadhonach: Middle (veean)
Moine: Mossland
Monadh: Mountains, moor
Mor, Mhor: Great
Odhar: Dappled, drab
Ord: Round or steep hill
Rathad: Road, way (rawud)
Riach, briach: Brindled, speckled
Ruadh: Reddish coloured
Ruadha: Promontory
Sgorr, Sgur: Sharp Peak
Sluggan: Gullet
Sneachda: Snow (snecta)
Sron: Point, ridge, nose
Stac: Steep rock
Stob: Point
Strath: Fertile valley
Tom: Mound, Knoll
Toul: Barn (towl)
Uaine: Green (wane)
Uisge: Water (whisky)

LUATH PRESS
GUIDES TO SCOTLAND

SOUTH WEST SCOTLAND. Tom Atkinson. A guide book to the best of Kyle, Carrick, Galloway, Dumfries-shire, Kirkcudbrightshire and Wigtownshire. This lovely land of hills, moors and beaches is bounded by the Atlantic and the Solway. Steeped in history and legend, still unspoiled, it is not yet widely known. Yet it is a land whose peace and grandeur are at least comparable to the Highlands.

Legends, history and loving description by a local author make this an essential book for all who visit -- or live in -- the country of Robert Burns.

ISBN 0 946487 04 9. Paperback. £3:50p.

THE LONELY LANDS. Tom Atkinson. A guide book to Inveraray, Glencoe, Loch Awe, Loch Lomond, Cowal, the Kyles of Bute, and all of Central Argyll.

All the glories of Argyll are described in this book. From Dumbarton to Campbeltown there is a great wealth of beauty. It is a quiet and a lonely land, a land of history and legend, a land of unsurpassed glory. Tom Atkinson describes it all, writing with deep insight of the land he loves. There could be no better guide to its beauties and history. Every visitor to this country of mountains and lochs and lonely beaches will find that enjoyment is enhanced by reading this book.

ISBN 0 946847 10 3. Paperback. Price £3:50p.

ROADS TO THE ISLES. Tom Atkinson. A guide book to Scotland's far north and west, including Ardnamurchan, Morvern,

Morar, Moidart, and all the west coast to Ullapool.

This is the area lying to the west and north of Fort William. It is a land of still unspoiled loveliness, of mountain, loch and silver sands. It is a vast, quiet land of peace and grandeur. Legend, history and vivid description by an author who loves the area and knows it intimately make this a book essential to all who visit this Highland wonderland.

ISBN 0 946487 01 4. Paperback. £3:50p.

THE EMPTY LANDS. Tom Atkinson. A guide book to the north of Scotland, from Ullapool to Bettyhill, and from Bonar Bridge to John O' Groats.

This is the fourth book in the series, and it covers that vast empty quarter leading up to the north coast. These are the Highlands of myth and legend, a land of unsurpassed beauty, where sea and mountain mingle in majesty and grandeur. As in his other books, the author is not content to describe the scenery (which is really beyond description) or advise you where to go. He does all that with his usual skill and enthusiasm, but he also places that superb landscape into its historical context, and tells how it and the people who live there have become what we see today. With love and compassion, and some anger, he has written a book which should be read by everyone who visits or lives in -- or even dreams about -- that empty land.

ISBN 0 946487 13 8. Paperback. £3:50p.

HIGHWAYS AND BYWAYS IN MULL AND IONA.
Peter Macnab. In this newly revised guidebook to Mull and Iona, Peter Macnab takes the visitor on a guided tour of the two islands. Born and grown up on Mull, he has an unparalleled knowledge of the island, and a great love for it. There could be no better guide than him to those two accessible islands of the Inner Hebrides, and no-one more able to show visitors the true Mull and Iona.
ISBN 0 946487 16 2. Paperback. £3:25p.

Other books on the Scottish countryside

WALKS IN THE CAIRNGORMS. Ernest Cross. The Cairngorms are the highest uplands in Britain, and walking there introduces you to sub-arctic scenery found nowhere else. This book provides a selection of walks in a splendid and magnificent countryside -- there are rare birds, animals and plants, geological curiosities, quiet woodland walks, unusual excursions in the mountains. Ernest Cross has written an excellent guidebook to those things. Not only does he have an intimate knowledge of what he describes, but he loves it all deeply, and this shows. **This is a companion volume to the present book.**

ISBN 0 946487 09 X. Paperback. £3:25p.

THE SPEYSIDE HOLIDAY GUIDE. Ernest Cross. Toothache in Tomintoul? Golf in Garmouth? Whatever your questions about Speyside, Ernest Cross has the answer in this Guide Book. Speyside is Scotland's ideal holiday centre. It has everything from the sub-arctic heights of the Cairngorms to the seemingly endless -- and quiet -- beaches. With a great wealth of peaceful towns and villages, it also possesses vast empty and open spaces, delightful to walk, a treasure to be discovered.

Ernest Cross knows and loves it all. In this book he directs you and guides you to the best of it. With his usual incisive wit and language, he introduces you to Scotland's most interesting area, and ensures that everyone, whether visitor or resident, is enriched by learning its secrets.

ISBN 0 946487 27 8. Paperback. £4:95p.

MOUNTAIN DAYS AND BOTHY NIGHTS. Dave Brown and Ian Mitchell. The authors have climbed, walked and bothied over much of Scotland for many years. There could be no better guide to the astonishing variety of bothies, howffs and dosses on the Scottish hills. They were part of the great explosion of climbing in the Fifties and Sixties, and they write of this with first-hand knowledge, sympathy and understanding.

Fishgut Mac, Desperate Dan, Stumpy and the Big Yin may not be on the hills any more, but the bothies and howffs they used are still there. There was the Royal Bothy, paid for by the Queen herself after an encounter with a gang of anarchist, republican hill-climbing desperadoes. There was the Secret Howff, built under the very noses of the disapproving laird and his gamekeepers. There was the Tarff Hotel, with its Three Star A.A. rating. These, and many more, feature in this book, together with tales of climbs and walks in the days of bendy boots and no artificial aids.

ISBN 0 946487 15 4. Paperback. £5:95p.

OTHER BOOKS FROM LUATH PRESS

TALES OF THE NORTH COAST. Alan Temperley and the pupils of Farr Secondary School. In this collection of 58 tales, there is a memorial to the great tradition of Highland story-telling. Simply told and unadorned, these tales are wide-ranging -- historical dramas, fairy tales, great battles, ship-wreck and ghosts, Highland rogues -- they all appear in this gallimaufry of tales, many of which have been told and re-told for generations round the fireside.

In addition to the tales, Alan Temperley has collected together a series of contemporary writings about the Clearances of Strathnaver, a central feature of local history, and a tragedy whose effects are still felt and discussed.

ISBN 0 946487 18 9 Paperback. £5:95.

POEMS TO BE READ ALOUD. *A Victorian Drawing Room Entertainment.* Selected and with an Introduction by Tom Atkinson. A very personal collection of poems specially selected for all those who believe that the world is full of people who long to hear you declaim such as these. The Entertainment ranges from an unusual and beautiful *Love Song* translated from the Sanskrit, to the drama of *The Shooting of Dan McGrew* and *The Green Eye of the Little Yellow God*, to the bathos of *Trees* and the outrageous bawdiness of *Eskimo Nell.* Altogether, a most unusual and amusing selection.

ISBN 0 946487 00 6. Paperback. £3:00p.

HIGHLAND BALLS AND VILLAGE HALLS. G.W. Lockhart. There is no doubt about Wallace Lockhart's love of Scottish country dancing, nor of his profound knowledge of it. Reminiscence, anecdotes, social commentary and Scottish history, tartan and dress, prose and verse, the steps of the most important dances -- they are all brought together to remind, amuse and instruct the reader in all facets of Scottish country dancing. Wallace Lockhart practices what he preaches. He grew up in a house where the carpet was constantly being lifted for dancing, and the strains of country dance music have thrilled him in castle and village hall. He is the leader of the well known *Quern Players*, and he composed the dance *Eilidh MacIain*, which was the winning jig in the competition held by the Edinburgh Branch of the Royal Scottish Country Dance Society to commemorate its sixtieth anniversary.

This is a book for all who dance or who remember their dancing days. It is a book for all Scots.

ISBN 0 96487 12 X Paperback. £3:95p.

THE CROFTING YEARS. Francis Thompson. A remarkable and moving study of crofting in the Highlands and Islands. It tells of the bloody conflicts a century ago when the crofters and their families faced all the forces of law and order, and demanded a legal status and security of tenure, and of how gunboats cruised the Western Isles in Government's classic answer. Life in the crofting townships is

described with great insight and affection. Food, housing, healing and song are all dealt with. But the book is no nostalgic longing for the past. It looks to the future and argues that crofting must be carefully nurtured as a reservoir of potential strength for an uncertain future.

Frank Thompson lives and works in Stornoway. His life has been intimately bound up with the crofters, and he well knows of what he writes.

ISBN 0 946487 06 5. Paperback. £5:95p.

TALL TALES FROM AN ISLAND. Peter Macnab. These tales come from the island of Mull, but they could just as well come from anywhere in the Highlands and Islands. Witches, ghosts, warlocks and fairies abound, as do stories of the people, their quiet humour and their abiding wit. A book to dip into, laugh over, and enthuse about. Out of this great range of stories a general picture emerges of an island people, stubborn and strong in adversity, but warm and co-operative and totally wedded to their island way of life. It is a clear picture of a microcosmic society perfectly adapted to an environment that, in spite of its great beauty, can be harsh and unforgiving.

Peter Macnab was born and grew up on Mull, and he knows and loves every inch of it. Not for him the 'superiority' of the incomer who makes joke cardboard figures of the island people and their ways. He presents a rounded account of Mull and its people.

ISBN 0 946487 07 3. Paperback. £6:50p.

BARE FEET AND TACKETY BOOTS. Archie Cameron. The author is the last survivor who those who were born and reared on the island of Rhum in the days before the First World War, when the island was the private playground of a rich absentee landowner. Archie recalls all the pleasures and pains of those days. He writes of the remarkable characters, not least his own father, who worked the estate and guided the Gentry in their search for stags and fish. The Gentry have left ample records of their time on the island, but little is known of those who lived and worked there. Archie fills this gap. He recalls the pains and pleasures of his boyhood. Factors and Schoolmasters, midges and fish, deer and ducks and shepherds, the joys of poaching, the misery of MacBraynes' steamers -- they are all here.

This book is an important piece of social history, but, much more, it is a fascinating record of a way of life gone not so long ago, but already almost forgotten.

ISBN 0 946487 17 0. Paperback. £6:25p

ON THE TRAIL OF ROBERT SERVICE. G.W.

Lockhart. It is doubtful if any poet, except perhaps Robert Burns, has commanded such world-wide affection as Robert Service. It is doubtful if any verse has been recited more often than *The Shooting of Dan McGrew* and *The Cremation of Sam McGee.* Boy Scouts, learned Professors, armchair wanderers and active followers of the open road have all fallen under the spell of the man who chronicled the story of the Klondike Gold Rush. Too few know the story of the Scottish bank-clerk who became the Bard of the Yukon -- his early revolt against convention, his wandering vagabond years in the States and Canada, and his later travels in Tahiti and Russia.

This book tells the story of a man who captivated the imagination of generations, expressed the feelings and emotions of millions, and painlessly introduced countless numbers to the beauties of verse. Written with the full support of his family and containing some hitherto unpublished photographs, this book will delight Service lovers in both the Old World and the New.

ISBN 0 946487 24 3 Price: £5:95

THE BOTHY BREW. Hamish Brown. Hamish Brown is well

known as a writer on Scottish, travel and outdoor subjects, as a photographer, lively lecturer, and editor of two poetry anthologies. His short stories have appeared in a wide range of publications.

He has climbed and travelled extensively in the Alps and less-known areas of Europe as well as in the remote Andes and Himalayas and each year spends some months in the south of Morocco. When not busy travelling and writing, home is at Kinghorn, with a view over the Forth to Edinburgh.

Although already the author of a dozen or so books, most of them reflecting his interest in and concern for the outdoors of Scotland, this is Hamish Brown's first collection of short stories.

This collection shows a remarkable range of interests and enthusiasms. They range from a murder on a beach at midnight to a family picnic at Loch Lomond, from a search for Painted Ladies in the mountains of Morocco to a search for a cuckoo in the Scottish hills.

These stories, although easy and a delight to read, yet show Hamish Brown's deep love for Scotland and the hills, and his profound knowledge of Scotland today.

ISBN 0 946 487 26 X. Paperback. Price: £5:95p.

COME DUNGEONS DARK. John Caldwell.

The Life and Times of Guy Aldred, Glasgow Anarchist. Hardly a street-corner site in Glasgow did not know Guy Aldred's great resonant voice belabouring the evils of society. Hardly a Glasgow voter for three generations did not have the opportunity of electing him to the city or national government he despised so much, and vowed to enter only on his own terms if elected. But he never was elected, although he once stood simultaneously for fourteen city wards. He claimed there was better company in Barlinnie Prison (which he knew well) than in the Corridors of Power.

Guy Alfred Aldred was born on November 5th 1886, and died on 16th October 1963. He had just 10 pence in his pocket when he died. Boy-preacher, Social Democrat, Prisoner of Conscience, Conscientious Objector, Anarcho-Communist, orator, writer, publisher -- Guy Aldred never ceased struggling for those things in which he believed. He was part of Glasgow's history, and must never be forgotten.
ISBN 0 946487 19 7. Paperback. Price £6:95p.

REVOLTING SCOTLAND. Jeff Fallow

A book of cartoons, showing Scotland of yesterday and today.
GREETINGS FRAE BONNY SCOTLAND!
Yes, but which Scotland?
Definitely not the Scotland of Heilan' Flings, Porridge and Haggis.
Certainly not the Scotland of Kilty Dolls, Mean Jocks and Tartan Trivia.
This is Scotland as it is, and Scotland as it was, and Scotland as it will be.
It is a book of cartoons, some very funny, some very bitter, and all very true.
You might learn more about Scottish history from these cartoons than you ever did at school.
If you are a visitor, you will understand more. If you are a Scot, you might just feel like getting up and doing something about it.

ISBN 0946487 23 1. Paperback. 130 pages. Price £5:95p.

SEVEN STEPS IN THE DARK. Bob Smith. The life and times of a Scottish miner. Before it is too late, before the last Scottish miner has hung up his lamp for the last time, Bob Smith has recorded his lifetime's work in the mines of Scotland. He started work in the pit when he was fourteen, working with his father, when every ton of coal was cut by hand with a pick, when ponies dragged it to the shaft, and every penny of pay was fought for against a grasping coal-owner.

He saw his industry nationalised, then mechanised, and finally destroyed. He worked in the pits for forty years, until injury forced his retirement. He was an active Tades Unionist all his life, and a Lodge Official for many years. He experienced strikes, and was always at the sharp end of the struggle for safety and better conditions. This is a miner's view of history, and records the reality behind the statistics and the rhetoric of politicians and managers and Trades Union officials.

ISBN 0 946487 21 9   Price: £8:95p.

Any of these books can be obtained from your bookseller, or, in case of difficulty, please send price shown, plus £1 for post and packing, to:

LUATH PRESS LTD.

BARR, AYRSHIRE. KA26 9TN

Tel: Barr (046-486) 636